Praise for *The Making of the Supply Chain*

"*The Making of the Supply Chain* confirms for both current and future supply chain professionals that they must never stop learning or innovating (embracing technology uninhibitedly) and never ever stop investing in themselves."

—Rob Haddock, transportation advisor, Albedo Logistics
Solutions; former group director of transportation strategy,
the Coca-Cola Company

"Remko van Hoek thoughtfully shares the history of trailblazing pioneers who helped shape the world we live in today. This read reminds us that innovation continues to revolutionize supply chains."

—Dr. Donna Palumbo-Miele, founder and CEO,
Concordia Supply Chain Group

"Remko van Hoek takes us behind the scenes of establishing the CSCMP Supply Chain Hall of Fame, an inspired initiative that honors innovators and leaders who have advanced the field. Remko uses the stories of five Hall of Famers to reveal the fundamental principles that have driven success in supply chain management. Filled with insight and inspiration, the book encourages readers to draw lessons from these pioneers and find ways to solve problems, drive progress, and make their own contributions to shape the future of the industry. *The Making of the Supply Chain* deserves a place on the bookshelves of all those passionate about advancing this critical and ever-evolving discipline."

—Matthew Waller, dean emeritus, Sam M. Walton College
of Business, University of Arkansas; 2020 CSCMP
Distinguished Service Award recipient

The Making of the Supply Chain

Lessons from the Past.
Insights for a Better Future.

The Making of the Supply Chain

How Five CSCMP Supply Chain Hall of
Famers Shaped the Industry

Remko van Hoek

Fayetteville | 2024

Manufactured in the United States of America

978-1-954892-13-2 (cloth)
978-1-954892-15-6 (e-book)

28   27   26   25   24   5   4   3   2   1

⊛ The paper used in this publication meets the minimum requirements of the American National Standard for Permanence of Paper for Printed Library Materials Z39.48-1984.

Library of Congress Control Number: 2024903861

Cover and chapter-opener image credits: Shipping trucks in Jakarta, Indonesia, courtesy of Tom Fisk via Pexels. Engraving of George Stephenson from *Lives of the Engineers* by Samuel Smiles, public domain. Henry Ford, courtesy of the Henry Ford Museum. George Laurer, courtesy of Wikimedia Commons. Elizabeth Dole, courtesy of the Robert J. Dole Institute of Politics. Johnnie Bryan Hunt, courtesy of the J. B. and Johnelle Hunt Family.

Resplendent and unfading is wisdom,
and she is readily perceived by those who love her,
and found by those that seek her.
—Book of Wisdom 6:12

The greatest among you must be your servant.
Whoever exalts himself will be humbled;
but whoever humbles himself will be exalted.
—Matthew 23:11–12

For Maryl, Ticho, Dylan, and Jason,
with thanks for your love

Contents

Foreword

The Path to a Better Way

The best way I can show my appreciation for *The Making of the Supply Chain* and all it has to offer its readers is by starting with a story about the book's author, Remko van Hoek.

Our paths crossed in a particularly meaningful way back in 2013 when we both were members of the board for the Council of Supply Chain Management Professionals. I was also in the middle of a long career with Monsanto, but I was transitioning from a senior director role in operations to vice president of global procurement strategy. Remko, meanwhile, was a global procurement director for PwC, and therefore someone I sought out for advice.

When I told him about my career shift into global sourcing and procurement, Remko immediately asked if I was familiar with the ideas behind SRM—supplier relationship management.

"I'd love to know more about it," I said.

"I'll not only tell you about it," he said, "I'm going to give you some of the work that I did. This can get you off on a really solid footing, and you will have a better chance of being successful. If you are, then even better things will happen for Monsanto. So I'd love to share those with you."

In short order, Remko sent me two long PDF documents he had created for PwC that, by the way, are still widely in use across the industry. And he continued to pour himself into my success. If there was anything I needed, he got it for me. Not only did he send me information and wish me the best of luck, but he was there to answer my questions, all without asking for anything in return.

As I see it, sharing lessons from Supply Chain Hall of Famers in a book is more than just a significant contribution to our discipline—although it certainly is that. It's also an interesting embodiment of the mastermind behind the project.

Remko cares deeply about the contributions he makes to everyone he meets and about his personal reputation, so he consistently does the right things for others in some magnificent ways. And like the select group of CSCMP Hall of Fame inductees featured in this book, Remko is always looking for opportunities to show people—not just tell them—how they might do things differently and better so they can achieve better outcomes.

The five innovators featured in this book—George Stephenson, Henry Ford, George Lauer, Elizabeth Dole, and J. B. Hunt—had no idea how their work would radically transform supply chains across the globe, but they, too, were seeking better ways of doing things. And then they shared those better ways with others to help make a better world.

That's why Remko helped me in my career transition. That's why he has served faithfully on the CSCMP board. That's why he led the effort for a physical home for the CSCMP Hall of Fame. That's why he does research and teaches university students and executive education courses. And that's why he wrote this book.

He knows the greats have something to teach us about doing things a better way.

These are five of the greatest of the greats, mind you. The CSCMP Hall of Fame honors innovators in two ways. Contributors to our field automatically join the hall when they receive the CSCMP Distinguished Service Award. It takes consistent and extraordinary contributions to earn that honor. Others have the unique distinction of a direct Hall of Fame nomination that's voted on by our membership. The contributions of these pioneers are not only significant, but game changing in their impact on the way things get done in supply chains. This book focuses on five of those inductees.

George Stephenson revolutionized rail transportation with innovative routes and standardizations. Henry Ford's assembly line concept helped automate supply lines and manufacturing lines that once were 100 percent peoplecentric. George Laurer developed a code for scanning technology that is so ubiquitous we can hardly imagine how we bought products without it. Elizabeth Dole created opportunities for women to lead and developed policies that make roads safer for everyone involved in the transportation of goods, not to mention the consumers who share the highways, skyways, rivers, and rails. And J. B. Hunt created a revolutionary partnership for intermodal transportation that maximizes efficiencies while putting less stress on the environment.

Remko highlights the stories of these pioneers with research and analysis that identifies how they got to their Hall of Fame innovations, explains why it matters to the supply chain profession, inspires us to pursue something greater than ourselves, and equips us with lessons that will help us get there. This moves in lockstep with the mission that drives CSCMP—developing, educating, and connecting supply chain practitioners and leaders throughout their careers.

We need to highlight the examples of the greats who came before us with breakthrough ideas for supply chain management so that others can see what it takes to go beyond the ordinary and achieve something truly great. We need supply chain leaders who think about different ways to realize new outcomes and who won't settle for making the same things happen over and over. We need innovative thought leaders who breathe life into transformational ideas, because that is how we continue the journey of improvement.

Remko's work—this book and everything else he does—honors the past while inspiring, educating, and equipping leaders of the future to break new ground and create what doesn't yet exist. Some readers of this book will no doubt develop ideas worthy of the hall of fame, and, of course, CSCMP will have a spot for them. Maybe they'll even appear in a future edition of this book. Because it's always a good time to show the world a better way.

Mark Baxa
President and CEO, CSCMP
President and CEO, FerniaCreek, LLC

Preface

Learning from the Best, Inspiring the Next

The idea for creating a Supply Chain Hall of Fame originated in 2016 during a board meeting for the Council of Supply Chain Management Professionals, more commonly known in the industry as CSCMP.

Brain Hancock, who at the time was an executive vice president of the Kansas City Southern Railway, argued that the discipline had sufficiently matured to be worthy of its own Hall of Fame. There were many innovators and leaders in supply chain who deserved celebrating and honoring, he said, and some innovations deserved more acknowledgment from the general public than they were receiving. Supply chains make the world of commerce go around, and, in those days before the COVID-19 pandemic, they tended to do so in the background. A Hall of Fame would not only honor innovators but also raise awareness about the discipline.

The board of directors, of which I was a member, wholeheartedly agreed, and we went to work on the particulars. The purpose of the CSCMP Supply Chain Hall of Fame, we decided, is to shine a bright light on the greatest innovations and leadership accomplishments in supply chain management, to learn from them, and to hopefully inspire further innovations and accomplishments, maybe even future Hall of Famers.

The next decision was easy. CSCMP already gave out an annual Distinguished Service Award (DSA) as its ultimate lifetime achievement honor. The list of DSA recipients included many founding fathers of the discipline from industry and academia, as well as such transformational leaders as Fred Smith of FedEx, Lee Scott of Walmart, and Ann Drake of DSC Logistics. So, the board decided to automatically include past and future DSA winners in the Hall of Fame.

Then came a more difficult issue. What would the Hall of Fame actually be? We decided to launch the Hall as an annual conference event, introducing new inductees with a ceremony, and then "house" the Hall on the CSCMP website. This was partially due to budget reasons but also, frankly, because the board was not certain the Hall of Fame would be a success.

Those concerns were quickly put to rest. Johnelle Hunt, the cofounder of J.B. Hunt Transport Services, addressed the conference in 2016, accepting her late husband's induction as an inaugural Hall of Famer, together with Henry Ford and Mr. Hunt's friend Malcom McClean. Her acceptance speech lit a fire in the audience of several thousand supply chain professionals from around the world. The board of directors, sitting in the front row in the room, knew we had a success on our hands—a valuable service to the profession and those who are involved in it.

Fast forward three years. After more than a decade on the board of directors, I was serving in my final year and, as outgoing board chair, I decided to issue a challenge: The CSCMP Supply Chain Hall of Fame was a proven success, a service to the profession, and a value to CSCMP's membership, I told the board. It deserved to be more than a conference event. The Hall of Fame needed a physical home.

Several board members said, "Yes, and good luck."

So I ran with it.

Fortunately, by this time I had moved to Northwest Arkansas, returning to academia from industry to teach supply chain management at the University of Arkansas and to coach and consult businesses. This gave me the opportunity to meet Mrs. Hunt again and to work with her organization on a proposal to UA's Sam M. Walton College of Business and to CSCMP.

Gus Blass III, a general partner of Capital Properties, and Alex Blass, a partner in Sage Partners, were working with Mrs. Hunt on a new office building development, and they generously offered to devote the top floor to the Hall of Fame, building it, fitting it out, and supporting the operation of the space.

My pitch to Matt Waller, who at the time was dean of the Walton College, was easy: Can we host the CSCMP Supply Chain Hall of Fame as a service to that organization and the supply chain profession?

His instant response: "It would be great if you can pull that off!"

I ran with it, and Dean Waller ended up featuring the story of bringing, building, and opening the Hall of Fame on an episode of his podcast about the history of the college,[1] and he listed it as one of the top ten accomplishments that occurred during his time as dean.[2]

The proposal to CSCMP became a bit more of a journey; service to a professional association doesn't always mean selfless service for everybody. But with the servant leadership of Rick Blasgen (then the CEO) and Mark Baxa (the board chair at the time), it all came together.

In my excitement about building and fitting out the space, I frequently shared design ideas with my wife, Maryl. And every time I brought something up, she was quick to suggest a much better approach. So I asked her if she could please help design and develop the place. There is hardly any person who walks through the doors of the Hall of Fame for the first time who isn't blown away by how special the place is. Again, all of this was made possible by the generosity of Mrs. Hunt and the Blass family.

By the way, it's worth noting that I might not have even made it to Arkansas if I hadn't listened to Maryl. "As long as I have known you," she had said before we first visited Arkansas, "you have always said that at some point you are going back to academia. When are you going to stop talking about that?" She never steers me wrong.

When the time approached to open the Hall of Fame, we held a trial board meeting there that included our children and the children of the Shemins, our dear friends who have helped make many special things possible and who have done, and do, so much for our family.

Everything was perfect, and we planned a big event for the opening. But because of the pandemic, we had to open the space virtually and were

---

1. Matt Waller, "Episode 150: History of the Walton College," November 24, 2021, in *Be EPIC Podcast*, 37:25, https://walton.uark.edu/be-epic-podcast/episodes/history -of-the-walton-college.php.

2. Matt Waller, "Episode 239: Reflecting on a Successful Tenure as Dean with Matt Waller," interview with Brent Williams, August 9, 2023, in *Be EPIC Podcast*, 43:06, https://walton.uark.edu/be-epic-podcast/episodes/reflecting-on-a-successful-tenure -as-dean-with-matt-waller.php.

unable to host many people in person for the opening exhibit devoted to Henry Ford.

As the COVID restrictions began to lift, Sarah Johnson, property manager for Sage Partners, became very busy patiently scheduling and supporting events at the Hall of Fame—CSCMP Roundtable meetings, classes of our Walton College supply chain master's degree program, supply chain conferences for Women Impacting Supply Chain Excellence (WISE) and the Supply Chain Management Research Center, procurement classes for Walmart International buyers, work sessions for Walmart International's supply chain teams, and meetings of Dean Waller's executive advisory board.

The CSCMP Roundtable made the Hall of Fame its home for its standing member meetings, and the International Supplier Collaboration Board, the regional airport authority, and many others have let the Hall of Fame host and inspire them during working sessions and meetings.

That is just the start. In addition to offering a location for the celebration of the greatest innovators in supply chain management, the Supply Chain Hall of Fame offers space for exhibits that are also shared through our website (walton.uark.edu/departments/supplychain/hall-of -fame/) and featured in publications.

The many lessons from our service and our research for the Hall of Fame led to the writing of this book. Academics need to serve society with insights and teachings from their work that can help drive progress and equip those who drive progress. The aspiration of this book is that it may make a modest contribution.

The academic founding fathers of the supply chain, Distinguished Service Award recipients, and former teachers of mine such as Martin Christopher and Don Bowersox all stand strong today as role models in that regard. They engaged with industry to learn, and they documented and researched pathways for progress in areas of supply chain innovation and practice where progress was needed. That links them closely to behaviors of Hall of Famers from industry, and it has helped explain much of their incredible impact on the body of knowledge in academia and practice.

This is a model many academics living in the comfort of a caste-like tenure and academic promotion system seem to have forgotten. And it is a model many are moving away from today in pursuit of academic career requirements. Those who pursue career over contribution and those who hide behind and sustain the meritless elements and benefits of the tenure system in the United States should reflect on the lessons from our founding fathers. And they should be reminded that those who serve lead and that the last will be first.

This book shares lessons from five unique and very different Supply Chain Hall of Famers. But this is more than a history book. It also identifies and shares how these Hall of Famers are connected and similar in more ways than you might realize, and how they all teach fundamentals of supply chain management that will sustain the discipline a long way into the future. The aim is to share those insights and lessons with the supply chain profession at large and hopefully offer inspiration for the future.

This book, however, is not done. A wall in the CSCMP Supply Chain Hall of Fame is devoted to statements from today's students of supply chain management. Reading the aspirations and dreams of these leaders of the future is a massive encouragement. The future is bright and hiring managers had better get ready for the talent that is coming their way!

What are your dreams and aspirations? What contributions do you hope to make to supply chain management and the society that supply chains support? As the chapter about the future indicates, there is so much more to come, to discover, and to learn. Many more chapters will be written, and I can't wait to see where we go next!

The Making of the Supply Chain

The First Links in the Chain

Supply chain management is a relatively young discipline. In fact, the term "supply chain" did not make it into the Merriam-Webster dictionary until September 2022, when it was included along with 369 other words like "dumbphone" and "adorkable" (Merriam-Webster 2022). And supply chain management has only scratched the surface of what it can mean for industry, the society in which it operates, and the people who operate it.

One of the silver linings in the tragic storms of the COVID-19 pandemic is a wider recognition of the importance of supply chains, both by consumers and by business leaders.

The pandemic and the logistical disruptions that followed caused companies to navigate bottlenecks and scarcity by reconsidering where they buy from, doubling down on the technologies that helped improve their visibility into their supply base, and focusing on collaborating throughout the supply chain (not just with their customers but also with their suppliers and even the suppliers' suppliers). Those shifts came on top of existing challenges such as sustainability concerns, driver shortages, and disruptions of channels to market with the move to omni and hybrid models.

While consumers have incredible supply chain capabilities at their fingertips, typically as nearby as their "dumbphones," they have also come to realize that goods don't just magically appear on a store's shelf or at their doorstep. Rick Blasgen, former CEO of the Council for Supply Chain Management Professionals (CSCMP), used to say that putting a product in the hands of a consumer is not like when you flip a switch and a light goes on. A lot needs to happen in between, and a lot can go wrong.

With that realization has come a greater interest in supply chain education among incoming university students. It's not clear whether supply chain management is "adorkable," but it's certainly trending in a positive direction. Salaries in supply chain management are rising and predicted labor market increases are solid for years to come. The talent coming out of university programs holds tremendous promise—the future for supply chain management is encouraging and exciting, as the closing chapter covers in more detail.

But while the interest and energy around supply chains might seem new, the discipline, in practice if not in name, actually predates civilization and has been the secret behind amazing episodes throughout history.

Cave dwellers, for instance, dug pits to trap mammoths, and, after killing them, they would butcher and move some of the meat to storage while using the rest for more immediate consumption. The pyramids were built because the Egyptians figured out a way to make large stones and drag, push, and pull them into place. And Alexander the Great conquered land throughout Western Asia and Egypt by using the forward deployment of food and ammunition to accelerate the campaigns of his armies.

Because the practice of supply chain management goes far back in history, there is a great deal we can learn from innovators and leaders in the discipline. By studying the past, we can further develop our skill sets and collaborate with others to put those skills to good use and to advance the field.

The drive to learn and develop, coupled with the realization of the importance of supply chain as a unique field, led to academic specialization in the discipline and the creation of the Council of Supply Chain Management Professionals.

In this regard, the 1960s were big for supply chain management. At the time, supply chain concepts were covered to some degree in marketing publications, and academics typically were housed in marketing or operations management departments. There were no academic journals in which they could publish research to advance knowledge and impact industry. But in 1961 the *Transportation Journal* was launched, and the *Journal of Purchasing* (now the *Journal of Supply Chain Management*) followed in 1965. Three professors, Gordons Wills, Martin Christopher, and Bernard (Bud) LaLonde, started the *International Journal of Physical Distribution* (IJPD) in 1970.

In 1963, meanwhile, a group of educators, consultants, and managers met at the American Marketing Association conference and discussed the idea that physical distribution as a discipline deserved greater focus than just being seen as one of the Ps in the marketing mix (place, along with product, price, and promotion).

Don Bowersox was at the table. He was working in industry at the time but moved to Michigan State University shortly thereafter, ending up as one of the first deans of a business school with a supply chain background.

Bowersox served as an early role model for supply chain managers and academics in a way that became fundamental to CSCMP's service: He championed a deep engagement between industry and academia, service to the profession through CSCMP and through the development and education of talent, and the development and dissemination of relevant, impactful knowledge. It's a model he would continue to embody beyond his retirement, showing up to deliver keynote speeches and to excite and contribute to CSCMP throughout the decades until just before his passing in 2011.

Bowersox and the others in that group in 1963 formed the National Council of Physical Distribution Management (NCPDM), which later became the Council of Logistics Management (CLM) and then, in 2005, the Council of Supply Chain Management Professionals (CSCMP). This global professional association now has more than nine thousand members who can take advantage of its networking opportunities, research, and education. It connects, educates, and develops the world's supply chain professionals, and it is a fitting organization for helping the world celebrate and learn from the greatest innovators and leaders in the discipline.

CSCMP (and its predecessors) has a long history of recognizing the leaders who have shaped the discipline and its future. In 1965, the NCPDM began honoring individuals with its Distinguished Service Award, which is given annually to someone who "exemplifies significant, consistent, and career-long contributions to the development of the logistics and supply chain management disciplines" (CSCMP, n.d.). (See Appendix for a list of recipients.)

The CSCMP Hall of Fame inducted its first class in 2016 to recognize the achievements of the discipline's greatest innovators in three main categories—industry transformers (technology, business or process, and legislative and regulatory), knowledge creators and communicators (researchers, authors, journalists, and consultants), and industry leaders (practitioners and other industry leaders).

This book studies five very different CSCMP Supply Chain Hall of Famers—George Stephenson, Henry Ford, George Lauer, Elizabeth Dole, and J. B. Hunt. Their stories demonstrate how innovations in supply chain management have changed the world in which we live by reshaping how we attain our products and services.

Each chapter provides the background and context on the major innovation attributed to the Hall of Famer. But this is not a history book. The chapters go into supply chain principles and lessons learned that are exemplified in the respective innovation, how the innovation shaped or was shaped by other key innovations, and how it is likely to impact the future of supply chains. The focus on the future offers inspiration and direction for furthering the greatest innovations and leadership accomplishments in supply chain management.

While the focus is on five innovators, there also are references and examples from other Hall of Famers that help drive home the takeaways. And while those takeaways are many, here are thirteen overarching lessons distilled from what we learned:

1. Supply Chain Innovations Connect the World and Make It a Better Place

Stephenson helped create a railway industry that connected ports, towns, and communities to enable greater productivity and welfare.

Ford helped create an industry that that made cars available and affordable, creating jobs and employment for all along the way.

Hunt, along with other Hall of Famers such as Malcom McLean, James Casey, Fred Smith, and George Raymond, helped create technologies and transportation systems that enhanced productivity and enabled global commerce, connecting the world. Hunt's contributions to intermodal partnerships also reduced the environmental impact of transportation.

Dole helped create a more diverse, inclusive, and safe transportation industry.

John Menzie, founder of the American Logistics Aid Network (ALAN) and a 2021 Hall of Fame inductee, provides a role model for how all the capability that supply chains have to offer can help save lives and communities struck by disaster.

The point is clear—supply chains' significant contributions to sustainability go back to the roots of our greatest innovations and leadership accomplishments. It's no surprise that supply chains have such a recognized and critical role to play in environmental, social, and corporate governance (ESG) and sustainability today.

2. Being Humancentric Is Key; It Certainly Isn't about Technology

A goal of Lauer's bar code technology was to improve checkout productivity in stores, but it also removed boring work for store associates, reduced errors for customers, and created a much faster checkout process.

Ford organized the assembly line and the Ford production system around the workers, stressing that pretty much every person could be given a job with the help of work designed around the person's ability. He made focusing on worker safety and clean working conditions a critical focus of the work design. And he encouraged lifelong learning by his staff as a way to continue to drive improvements and development.

J. B. Hunt's leadership approach mostly focused on people and relationships, not technology. And Dole drove improvements for everyone in transportation with initiatives that improved safety and promoted opportunities and inclusion for women and disabled people.

3. Hall of Famers Did Not Come Up with Their Innovations

Lauer wasn't the first to come up with a bar code, and Ford didn't create the first or only assembly line in his day. Safety and the environment were not new topics at the Department of Transportation when Dole became its secretary. And Stephenson did not invent the railway.

What these Hall of Famers did was to get the innovations to work and build a sustainable system (the factory and the integrated supply chain in Ford's case, the industry and the complexities around it in the case of Stephenson) that could be institutionalized, replicated, and further improved upon.

4. Hall of Fame Innovations Do Not Stand on Their Own Legs

Lauer's bar code succeeded because there was an industry consortium spanning the retail supply chain involved that was ready to adopt the technology. And intermodal combines existing transportation modes and standardized containerization that came from Hall of Famer Malcom McClean.

Hall of Famers Taiichi Ohno and Eliyahu Goldratt developed methods to improve and optimize existing processes, not necessarily create new ones. Michael Dell uses customization for personal computers to create new customer value but requires traditional mass production of components to ensure affordability. And online shopping from Jeff Bezos requires a transportation network for delivery to get it to work for consumers.

5. Connections Make the Chain, Not the Parts

It is not the individual parts but their combination that makes the innovation work.

Intermodal combines containerization with rail and road transportation to offer a new transportation system. Dell's mass customization model hinges upon different configurations of existing PC parts. And Ohno and Goldratt fundamentally focused on process and flow optimization, not the individual parts of the supply chain. Ford integrated the supply chain vertically to drive reliability of availability and the opportunity to scale and manage for productivity. That was the key to producing affordable cars, not the assembly line on its own.

6. It Takes a Village

Stephenson's railway projects relied on an ecosystem of suppliers, sources, and technologies. And he had a locomotive factory, track patents, and relationships with financiers, leading experts, and fellow engineers and mechanics.

Ohno's lean production system is critically dependent upon carefully designed relationships and integrations of many suppliers, as explained in Hall of Famer Peter Drucker's outsourcing theory. Dell does the same in PCs, buying more than his company makes itself, and Amazon's marketplace is just that, an online marketplace that thrives based upon the presence of many vendors.

7. Setting Higher Standards Is Only the Start

The creation of the pallet, the sea container, the bar code, and the width of a rail track set new and higher standards in the supply chain. But that was not the purpose of any of those innovations. The purpose was to make the supply chain better by creating greater productivity, reliability, operability, and interoperability. It was how the standard was put to good use by supply chain managers that made the innovations world changing.

Note that this does not imply the need for 100 percent standardization. Rail tracks are not the same width everywhere in the world and bar codes are not used for all products.

8. Innovations and Innovators Are Never Done

Drucker spoke of logistics as the last dark continent (Drucker 1962), and we can easily argue that today we have, at best, a candlelit supply chain. There is still so much to learn, invent, solve, and improve by using and building upon Hall of Fame innovations.

Ohno and Goldratt offered continuous improvement approaches, and Ohno also built upon the Ford production system, improving the foundational innovation it provided.

The bar code is evolving into 3-D versions and connecting with related technologies such as blockchain to create additional value from the innovation.

Elizabeth Dole's ten-point plan for increasing the role of women in transportation maintains high relevance today, and experienced leaders will see opportunities to add elements to the plan and grow its impact on diversity and inclusion in the workplace.

J. B. Hunt continued to explore entrepreneurial opportunities until the last days of his life, and his wife and company cofounder, Johnelle Hunt, continues to do so. "I just want to make him proud and take forward what we started together," she has said (Hunt 2021).

9. Innovation Needs Failure

J. B. Hunt focused on his big dreams and long-term plans, forgiving missed quarterly goals along the way. Ford had an explicit focus on using lessons from failures to save time and money and on moving forward to other things that might work. Failure, bottlenecks, or suboptimization provided the basis for new technologies such as intermodal and the bar code. And it is where process optimization focuses its efforts to create new and greater value.

10. Hard Work and Relevance Are More Important than Grand Theories and Academic Science

IBM had brilliant engineers working on its bar code efforts, but Lauer went with a different approach that he thought was better. He went off script and worked on his own over the weekend while his boss was on vacation on a proposal that led the company in a new direction.

J. B. Hunt never went to college and drove trucks himself until he was forty. Giving up, even when the company was turning a loss and people advised closure, was not an option for him and his wife.

"We had to keep going and figure out a way to make it work," she said (Hunt 2021).

Supply chain management theory was heavily influenced by the Ford production model, not the other way around. Drucker's outsourcing theory was mostly practical and involved no mathematical modeling or complex structural equation modeling. It was a logical concept and approach that managers ran with. Goldratt was a consultant, not an academic, and he got fired from his first professional services job for focusing on the development of his process optimization approach.

11. Innovations Keep Giving

Stephenson's initial railroad efforts were in the days when rail was used to carry coal out of mines. His projects connected mines to ports and then communities to each other, eventually creating a transportation network that helped change the economy and society based upon the power of transportation.

Rail also was part of the intermodal breakthrough achieved by J.B. Hunt Transport. Hunt's innovation initially was driven by transport optimization considerations but, as the triple bottom line concept teaches, some things that are good for profit also can be really good for the planet and for people (Mena et al. 2021). Intermodal remains one of the most environmentally friendly means of transportation because it removes trucks from the road and puts containers on railways. It also is one of the best ways to battle driver shortages in the transportation sector.

The bar code, meanwhile, improved retail checkout productivity and saved time for consumers. Today the bar code is used to track and trace products in many industries, and 3-D bar codes are used for information dissemination and secure transactions.

12. Comfort Zones Can Stifle Innovation

For innovation to flourish, supply chain managers must avoid getting hooked on strategies that work and deliver results. The COVID-19 pandemic taught us that pursuing a global sourcing strategy for cost savings too one-dimensionally and too universally exposes companies to large risks (van Hoek 2022). These risks can be traced back to staying in a proven swimming lane and comfort zone.

As tempting as it may be to continue using strategies and innovations that work, managers can never be excused from challenging the status quo and making every decision on its own merits. The very nature of lean production and the Ford production system, for example, is continuous improvement and optimization, not consistent adoption of the same template.

13. Supply Chain Innovations Should Be Seen for Their Societal Impact Agenda

Many supply chain innovations still have much more to give to society and are being challenged to do so. European legislation about third-party compliance and supply chain transparency is forcing companies to improve visibility up and down their supply chains, into tier-two and tier-three suppliers. While this is nothing that theory does not aspire to, it is legislation that is forcing progress in industry.

Regulators targeting the supply chain also achieve legislative reach far beyond the geographic scope of the legislative authority. All this implies that supply chains are more of a lever for societal impact and progress than perhaps traditionally considered in industry and theory.

Every effort to decouple Russian suppliers and sources from the global supply chain in response to Russia's war against Ukraine illustrates the potential of using supply chain disintegration as a force for good and for making ESG efforts very real and complete (Srai et al. 2023). Turning supply chain thinking around by 180 degrees (disintegration over integration and decoupling over aligning) provides a new lens for supply chains as a force for societal progress and good.

As you can see, Supply Chain Hall of Famers offer a number of leadership lessons and approaches to innovation that we can apply going forward. Supply chains, after all, are about getting things from here to there in the most efficient, economical ways. So let's dive in and learn more about what George Stephenson, Henry Ford, George Lauer, Elizabeth Dole, and J. B. Hunt can teach us about taking the discipline from where it was to where it's going.

References

CSCMP. n.d. "Distinguished Service Award." https://cscmp.org/CSCMP/Awards/Distinguished_Service_Award.aspx.

Drucker, Peter F. 1962. "The Economy's Dark Continent." *Fortune*, April, 103, 265, 268, 270.

Hoek, Remko van. 2022. "Lessons Learned—Lessons Enacted? Opportunities for Supply Chain Improvements Coming out of the Pandemic." *Medical Research Archives* 10, no. 12 (December 2022). https://esmed.org/mra/article/view/3398.

Hunt, J. 2021. 33rd Annual Arkansas Business of the Year ceremony, where Johnelle Hunt was given a Legacy of Leadership Award. March 10. YouTube video, 5:24. https://youtu.be/6-zciagYL58?si=0fFKDhU1q8rhfV8W.

Mena, C., R. van Hoek, and M. Christopher. 2021. *Leading Procurement Strategy.* London: Kogan Page.

Merriam-Webster. 2022. "We Added 370 New Words to the Dictionary for September 2022." https://www.merriam-webster.com/words-at-play/new-words-in-the-dictionary.

Srai, Jagjit Singh, Gary Graham, Remko van Hoek, Nitin Joglekar, and Harry Lorentz. 2023. "Impact Pathways: Unhooking Supply Chains from Conflict Zones—Reconfiguration and Fragmentation Lessons from the Ukraine-Russia War." *International Journal of Operations & Production Management* 43, no. 13, 289–301. https://doi.org/10.1108/IJOPM-08-2022-0529.

George Stephenson

Birth: June 9, 1781
Died: August 12, 1849 (age 67)
Company: Robert Stephenson and Company
Hall of Fame Induction: 2018
Key Supply Chain Innovation: Builder of the modern railway

The investors in a new coal-mining operation in northern England could not have been pleased when faulty equipment slowed the progress toward their profits.

The colliery, known as the Killingworth High Pit because it was near the village of Killingworth, opened in 1810 and almost immediately encountered an ongoing problem: The steam engine that pumped water from the mine shaft was a dud. It wasn't able to clear the pit of water and, therefore, the workers couldn't get to the bottom to extract the coal.

After more than a year of fruitless effort by the engine and failed attempts to repair it by the "enginemen" in the region, the operators of the mine decided to make a last-ditch effort by giving George Stephenson a shot at fixing it.

Stephenson was a twenty-nine-year-old brakeman, meaning that he operated the engine that lowered miners into the pit and brought them out again. He wasn't educated as an engineer or trained as a mechanic. But he had a reputation for making practical repairs on just about anything—from shoes to watches to steam engines—and he claimed he could fix the pump.

"I could alter her and make her draw," Stephenson had said after inspecting the engine. "In a week's time from this I could send you to the bottom" (Smiles 1857).

Knowing that the professionals had failed for months and would greet his efforts with reservations, if not outright hostility, Stephenson assembled his own team that took the engine apart. They doubled the size of the injection cap, shortened the length of the cylinder, and made a few other rough alterations before putting it back together four days later. Then they put their work to the test in the coal mine.

"It was kept pumping all Thursday," according to Stephenson biographer Samuel Smiles, "and by Friday afternoon the pit was cleared of water, and the workmen were 'sent to the bottom,' as Stephenson had promised" (Smiles 1857).

The successful repair earned Stephenson a modest bonus in his next paycheck, but it also led to his promotion to "engineman" and, in 1812, to "engine-wright," putting him in charge of all the colliery's machinery. The turning-point story also illustrates how Stephenson used his work ethic, grit, ingenuity, and passion for solving challenges to rise from his hardscrabble working-class roots and position himself to become the history-making father of the modern railway.

Stephenson's transformative influence on rail transportation is much like Henry Ford's influence on supply chain production. Just as Ford did not invent the assembly line, Stephenson did not invent the key elements to the public railway.

Hunter Davies, the prolific Scottish-born author who is best known for writing the only authorized biography of the Beatles, covered Stephenson and the history of railways in a 1975 book, in which he pointed out that "three elements came together to form what we now know as railways and George Stephenson invented none of them" (1975). The three elements referenced by Davies were the wheel, the track, and the power source. Stephenson also often gets credit for the locomotive, but he never claimed such recognition. As Robert Stephenson, his son and business partner, noted, "The locomotive is not the invention of one man, but of a nation of mechanical engineers" (Smiles 1857).

George Stephenson, however, did bring these elements and several others together into a breakthrough system application that produced a commercially viable public railway system that changed the way raw materials, finished goods, and passengers were transported across the globe.

"He gathered together the scattered threads of ingenuity which already existed and combined them into one firm and complete fabric of his own," Smiles (1857) wrote. "He realised the plans which others had imperfectly formed; and was the first to construct, what so many others had unsuccessfully attempted, the practical and economical working locomotive."

Stephenson engineered several related aspects of the modern railway, including the use of fences and sleepers, bridges and tunnels. And one of the most important foundations Stephenson laid was to set the gauge standard at 4 feet, 8.5 inches. This standard, which is still used in many countries around the world, enabled interoperability between different railways and the eventual creation of a national and international railway network.

Railways not only made products such as coal more widely available and more affordable to consumers but also accelerated communication via mail and gave farmers new and wider market access, raising food standards. Additionally, the demand for public transportation was large, which drove high returns on the investments in the railways, fueling investor appetite for more projects.

Stephenson also helped his son, Robert, start a locomotive factory that ended up exporting engines throughout the world, and he jointly patented iron rails. Not only did this help enable the Industrial Revolution, but new professions and jobs were created in this process, most notably the "navvies" who built and laid the rails. These workers experienced a growing job market that quickly became international, and many navvies from the United Kingdom traveled to projects in countries like France and Canada.

Stephenson, in short, set new standards, created new roles and professions, and helped create and grow an ecosystem of stakeholders, suppliers, industries, investors, and legislators. He also expanded the use of his innovations far beyond their initial region, industry, and supply chain segment of application, enabling the Industrial Revolution to flourish and change the world forever.

The Birth of an Industry

Wikipedia's entry for George Stephenson describes him as a "British civil engineer and mechanical engineer," which could leave the impression that he spent much of his early life with his face buried in books and then studied for years at some prestigious university. But Stephenson didn't attend college. In fact, he didn't even learn to read and write until he was in his late teens when he had saved enough money from his day jobs to fund classes at night schools.

His investment paid off by feeding his hunger to learn new things and increasing his opportunities to apply his natural inclination for engineering. It was those skills that led to his opportunity to fix the pump at Killingworth High Pit. And the more responsibility he was given, the more he worked to solve one of the biggest challenges of the coal industry—how to efficiently and effectively move heavy loads across long distances.

Horse-drawn wooden trucks running on wooden boards were used in German mining as far back as 1530. By the early seventeenth century, the mining industry had begun switching to wooden rails, and it would eventually adopt cast-iron rails in the 1770s (Davies 1975). Thomas

Newcomen produced the first steam pump in 1712, while James Watt perfected a steam engine that could turn wheels in 1782. Then, in 1801, Richard Trevithick completed the first locomotive—a steam engine that ran on its own power.

Trevithick's original locomotive chugged over unpaved roads and without a track. In 1804, he developed a second locomotive that ran on rails, but those rails were unable to handle the machine's weight. In 1808, he dropped the idea without having attempted either to invent a better track or reduce the weight of the engines. In 1812, however, John Blenkinsop built the first commercially successful locomotive and track and put them to use in a mine near Leeds, still years before Stephenson began work on the first public railway (Davies 1975).

Stephenson's breakthrough was bringing steam locomotive technology together with tracks and several other system elements to build the first public railway for coal transportation and the general public. He engineered a route, built a locomotive (Figure 2.1) known as "Loco motion No. 1" and a cart (the experiment), tracks (using malleable iron), and junctions (using cast iron), and worked with investors to get the project privately financed, litigated through Parliament, and into operation.

The first tracks on the nine-mile railway between Darlington and Stockton were laid on May 23, 1822, and the initial funding raised for the project was £120,000 (US$597,600) (Officer 2024). The line opened three years later on September 27, 1825, when 650 people, many hanging off the train, took part in the inaugural journey. The train weighed ninety tons and stretched four hundred feet with eleven wagons carrying coal, one with flour, seven with passengers, and fourteen for workers. When going downhill, it reached a top speed of a whopping fifteen miles per hour (Davies 1975).

After this, several other public railways followed. The Liverpool to Manchester line, for instance, was significant because it was the first inter-city railway (Davies 1975) and the first to use two-way tracks and signaling (Smiles 1857). The Liverpool line also moved the rail transportation services beyond coal mining and into cotton and mail transportation. Cotton was shipped to Liverpool from the United States and the train brought it to the mills of Manchester, connecting two different parts of the world in a more efficient, cost-effective, and faster manner than the alternatives of horse-drawn boats in canals or horse-drawn carriages.

FIGURE 2.1 Loco motion No. 1 used on the Darlington line

The No. 1. Engine at Darlington.

Source: Smiles 1868

The Darlington line was originally envisioned as a horse-drawn train. While Stephenson may have planned to switch to steam power all along, he did not pivot to the locomotive until long after he was hired to survey the route and develop a cost estimate and build plan. The move to the locomotive was driven not by self-interest but by a belief in the power of the technology. His argument was that a locomotive could do the work of many horses. A comparison (Figure 2.2) showed that the locomotive, even at very slow speeds, outperformed horses, and that this difference grows with accelerating speeds.

The development of a survey for a new line involved tendering bids on the project, market research, and a study of supplier pricing as part of the planning and budgeting process, very much as a modern supply chain program would be planned. In addition to raising financing for the project and setting up railway companies to operate the line, Stephenson needed acts of Parliament that approved the building of

FIGURE 2.2 Wood's 1825 comparison of locomotive power to horsepower

Velocity in miles per hour.	Weight conveyed in cwts.	Distance traversed in miles, being that which a horse performs in a day.	Resistance in lbs. upon an edge-rail-road, reckoning the friction equal to the 200th part of the weight.	Power which a horse exerts upon the load from formula $\frac{224}{v}$	Number of horses required to perform the work.	Weight conveyed in cwts. by a horse upon an edge-rail-road, by formula $\frac{400}{v}$	Weight which a loco-motive engine will drag upon an edge-rail road in cwts.	Ratio of performance of a loco-motive engine and horses, when the speed at which they travel is the same in each.	Time in hours occupied by horses in travelling 20 miles, at the respective velocities.	Distance in miles which a loco-motive engine would travel in the preceding time, going at the rate of 6 m. an hour.	Ratio of distance traversed by loco-motive engines and horses, in the same time.	Number of horses' work which a loco-motive engine would be continually performing in the time-column 10, travelling at the rate of 6 miles an hour, and horses at the respective rates of column 1.
2	800	20	448	112	4	200	800	4 : 1	10	60	3 : 1	12
3	800	20	448	74¾	6	133⅓	800	6 : 1	6⅔	40	2 : 1	12
4	800	20	448	56	8	100	800	8 : 1	5	30	1½ : 1	12
5	800	20	448	44⅘	10	80	800	10 : 1	4	24	1⅕ : 1	12
6	800	20	448	37⅓	12	66⅔	800	12 : 1	3⅓	20	1 : 1	12

Source: Wood 1825

the railway over competing surveyors and alternative builders and developers.

In May of 1824, Stephenson was commissioned as engineer for the Liverpool to Manchester line (more than a year before completing the Darlington line!), and his survey was done in February 1825. His estimated budget of £400,000 (US$1,932,000) was ripped to pieces in a parliamentary debate that lasted months. He was fired from the job, later rehired as a coengineer, and eventually ended up as sole engineer. The line opened in September 1830, five years after the initial survey.

Stephenson's collaboration with his son Robert was key to the development of the innovation and the industry. Robert Stephenson was the engineer on the first trunk railway between London and Birmingham. He also advanced the business model and managerial organization of projects by deputizing parts of a line so that he did not have to follow up on every detail (Bailey 2003).

Robert Stephenson also was the engineer of the Leicester and Swannington Railway, which opened in 1833. Other major lines across

FIGURE 2.3 Development of the railway industry in the UK 1844–1849

Year	Acts of Parliament for Railway Construction	Capital Authorised £million	Total Actual Capitalization £million	Miles in Operation
1844	48	17.8	72.3	2148
1845	120	60.8	88.4	2441
1846	270	136.0	126.1	3036
1847	190	40.3	166.8	3945
1848	85	4.6	200.4	5127
1849	34	3.1	230.0	6031

Source: Bailey, 1999

his large portfolio of projects were Derby to Leeds, Normantown to York, Manchester and Leeds, and Birmingham and Derby, and he took the railway industry into a rapid growth stage with interest from many regions, countries, and investors.

In October 1844, financier George Hudson was able to raise £2.5 million (US$12.15 million) for three lines without even disclosing any detail about them (Davies 1975). In 1846, £16.5 million (US$77.12 million) was spent on wages for two hundred thousand navvies. At this point the navvies represented a workforce larger than the British navy and the army combined. Soon they also traveled to other countries to help build railways, exporting their profession to France and Canada (Davies 1975), and the railway industry grew rapidly in the years to follow (Figure 2.3).

The impact on distribution grew in line with this expansion of the railways. Consider mail, for example: from 1839 to 1865, the number of chargeable letters carried by rail increased from 76 million to 720 million. And the mileage covered by mail trains in the United Kingdom increased from 25,000 per day in 1854 to 60,000 per day in 1867, or 240 percent (Smiles 1857).

Stephenson's Principles Exemplified

Several supply chain principles and lessons played a key role in the creation of the public railway. Most notably, they involve the fundamental concept of holistically connecting parts of the chain and elements of the system; the impact of supply across industries, regions, and countries; the enabling role of technology; and the importance of continued discovery and learning.

Connecting the parts to form the chain, Part I. Many of the engineers who came before Stephenson tended to concentrate on one side of locomotive making, and they gave up when ancillary problems arose (Davies 1975). Stephenson approached the railway holistically. He developed a locomotive, rails, and many other elements, and then he successfully brought them together in a working system.

Considering impact beyond the individual link and system part. Until 1825, locomotives were seen as a local phenomenon (Davies 1975)—a specialized means of transportation that was confined to coal mines. Stephenson broadened the use to include passenger transportation and several other industries, and he expanded railways into new regions, countries, and parts of the supply chain. He also thought beyond the main technologies, developing many adjacent aspects to getting the railway built and functioning, including fencing, signaling, bridges, and tunnels.

Connecting the parts to form the chain, Part II. The building of the first public railway with a steam engine locomotive did not just require the engineering of connected technologies and system elements; it also required an ecosystem of suppliers, companies, and financiers. The railways were privately funded, and a sector of builders and contractors emerged around the projects to build and supply rails, fences, sleepers, and even temporary housing for workers. Players in this ecosystem experienced profitable growth. Figure 2.4 shows the growth in locomotive production in the United Kingdom, and Figure 2.5 shows the margin and profitability of the R. Stephenson locomotive business.

Global scope and impact of the supply chain. By growing the impact of the railway into the cotton industry, Stephenson also provided a transportation link that connected American cotton farms to Manchester mills for a global flow of goods. When other countries started building railways, exports of technology, products, and workers began. Navvies started

FIGURE 2.4 Locomotive production for the UK and foreign markets

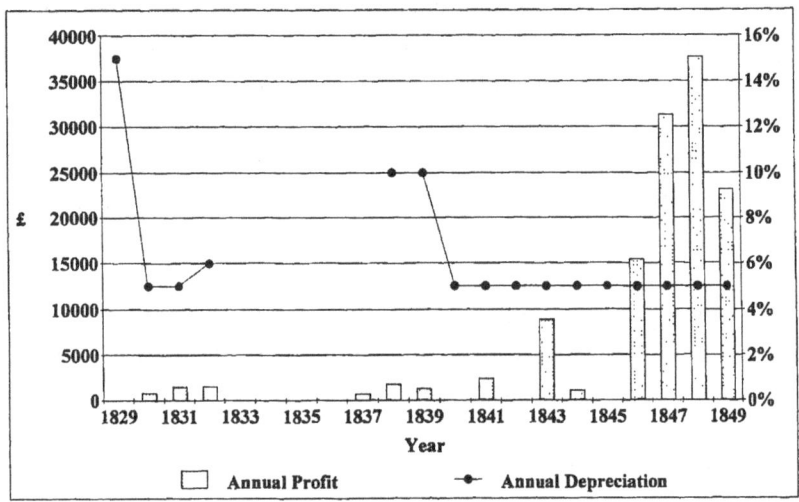

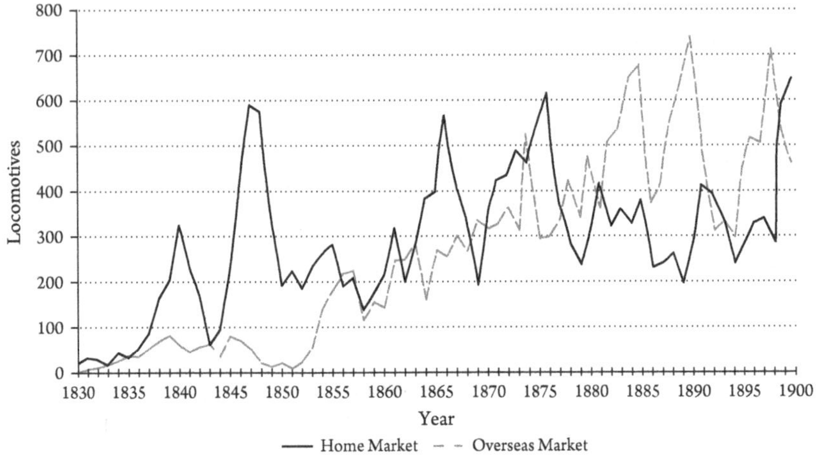

Source: Bailey 1999

FIGURE 2.5 Profitability of R. Stephenson & Company 1829–1849

Source: Bailey 1999

moving abroad for projects and the export of locomotives became a key driver of the industry's growth. (Figure 2.4 shows exports of locomotives from the UK.)

Economies of speed and scale. With the growth of the railway industry came opportunities to increase production and drive economies of scale

(Figure 2.6). A key part of the railways' contribution to business was more efficient and faster delivery. The greater access to coal was driven not just by its availability, but by the less expensive transportation provided by the railways. Greater access to farm produce was enabled by less expensive transportation and the fact that faster transportation reduced perishability risks.

Transportation enables industrialization, productivity, and wealth creation. The Industrial Revolution was truly revolutionary because of the dramatic changes it brought for mass production of goods and the creation of wealth that followed. The modern railway system enabled that revolution in several ways by its impact on the supply chain.

For starters, much of the Industrial Revolution was powered by coal, and the industry needed to accelerate the transportation of its products to factories to keep pace with production demands. Railways got coal to those factories faster, but also in a more cost-efficient manner. It also led to affordable consumer access to passenger transportation, and it then brought goods more efficiently to customers from around the world.

Consider alternative technologies and what they can add and complement. The railway proved to be a competitive alternative to horse-drawn carriages and canals, and it complemented existing ocean shipping routes between the United States and Liverpool.

Persistence and continuous discovery. Trevithick may have invented the locomotive, but he gave up on the technology early on. Stephenson's persistent pursuit of new discoveries began during his early mining days and continued as he developed the railway and its many parts.

Work on continuously improving parts of the system resulted, for example, in increased speeds of the trains. The original coal-hauling locomotives chugged along at four to six miles per hour. By the time the first passenger train began its route between Liverpool and Manchester, speeds had increased to an average of seventeen miles per hour. Before long, they had reached fifty to sixty miles per hour—"the pistons in the cylinders, at sixty miles, travelling at the inconceivable rapidity of 800 feet per minute!" (Smiles 1857).

FIGURE 2.6 Growth in locomotive batch size

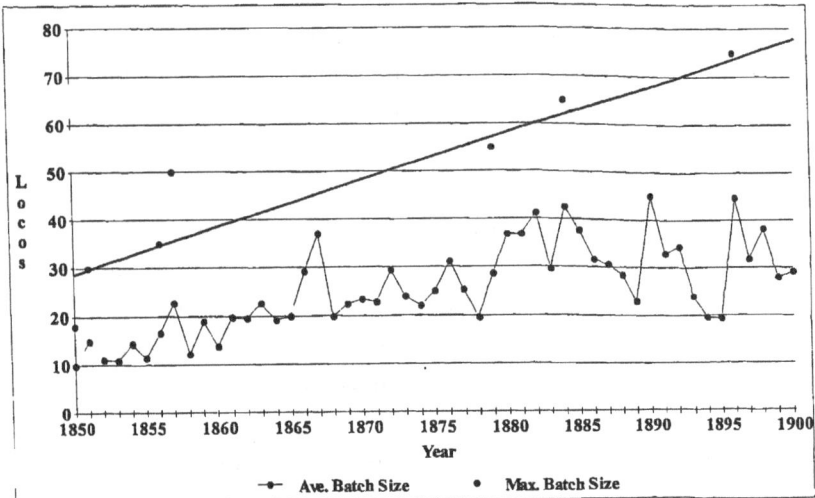

Source: Bailey, 1999

Key Lessons

The supply chain lessons from Stephenson's career aren't just found in the innovation (railways) and its impact on the marketplace. How he went about creating change and improvements also provides invaluable insights for today's supply chain innovators. For instance:

Transformation takes time and effort. One of the less frequently studied supply chain realities is that change can take a long time (van Hoek et al. 2010). The creation of the railways illustrates that a successful proof of concept doesn't equal adoption and that the adoption of technologies often is gradual.

It was twenty-two years after the first locomotive was built before Stephenson started work on the Darlington line. Building this line took two years, and other lines like the Liverpool line took years just to get started, including months of debate in Parliament.

Even after the opening of the Darlington line, horses continued to be used on that same line until 1833 (Davies 1975). And, as Figure 2.3 shows, it took nearly seven hundred acts of Parliament to get five thousand miles of railway in operation by 1848. At that point, there was still no nationwide network. The transformation required persistence on multiple aspects of the projects that eventually led to meaningful change.

A problem-solving mind-set turns theory into application. There is often a gap between the understanding of supply chain concepts and their application (van Hoek et al. 2020). Stephenson closed that gap with a problem-solving mentality that looked beyond the constraints of individual theories and academic ideas and focused more on a practical system that would bring about change.

For instance, a lot of the pieces of the railway technology where in existence when Stephenson started building the first railway, but he solved issues in ways that allowed those technologies to work together when he set operating standards, created new jobs and roles, made the case for financing, and came up with a detailed survey and build plan.

It has been said that Stephenson had a dislike for theoretical scientists from highly regarded London establishments, perhaps because of his struggle to become an engineer without academic credentials and education and perhaps because he wasn't always considered credible in those circles during his early days (Davies 1975). This chip on his shoulder seemed to serve him well in discovering a way to make railways a reality, despite the fact that he lacked the availability of scientific theory.

The right way is the best way to create supply chain success. For the Darlington line, Stephenson picked a type of rail that was not covered by his own patent and was against his own financial interests, because he believed that this technology was better suited for the project. This illustrates how individuals in the ecosystem sometimes need to act against their own perceived best interest for the greater good of the supply chain.

In the long run, not only did this pay off for the supply chain holistically, but it also opened a path to the long-lasting economic gain and growth of the railway industry, which benefited everyone in the industry.

Robert Stephenson also showed he was willing to put the long-term needs of the industry ahead of his short-term best interest. He was critical of the massive growth of railway projects in the early 1800's period of railway mania. While project requests came into his company by the dozen, he argued that the industry would not be able to drive returns on all the projects if it took on too much too soon (Ross 2010).

Links to Other Supply Chain Innovators

There's little doubting that George Stephenson was an inspiration to Henry Ford, which is one reason the Henry Ford Museum houses a replica of Stephenson's "Loco motion No. 1" model.

Interestingly, the application of rail and trains in Ford's supply chain mostly drew from Stephenson's mining roots. Rail was used inside the company and for very dedicated purposes, just as in the Ford production sites.

There also is a link to Robert Stephenson's philosophy that there are three requirements to having a successful machine: design, materials, and method of manufacturer (Bailey 2003). Henry Ford equally focused on tooling methods of manufacturing with and beyond the assembly line.

J. B. Hunt's development of truck-train intermodal partnerships, meanwhile, would not have been possible without the modern railway. Like that of Stephenson, Hunt's innovation advanced transportation technology with new capabilities that were interconnected with other modes of transportation. Just as Stephenson connected ocean shipping to the railway for bringing cotton from the United States to Liverpool, intermodal connected the railway to road transportation for final and incoming distribution of goods.

The importance of standard setting may appear to be a small note in the long list of Stephenson's accomplishments, but it is one that enabled interoperability of the many railway projects and eventually allowed for connecting national and international railway systems. Other standard setters in the Hall of Fame are George Lauer for setting the Universal Product Code (or UPC), Malcom McLean for developing the sea container, and George Raymond for creating the wooden pallet and pallet jack.

These standards enable supply chains to scale and connect across countries and companies, dynamically and efficiently, so that supply chain managers can focus not on making the connections but on leveraging across the connections.

Today's Relevance

The railway is a transportation mode, but the invention of the railway held implications for all parts of the supply chain (Table 2.1).

The roots of the railway in the coal industry came from the need to scale the mining and delivery of coal to fuel the Industrial Revolution. In addition to that, the case for the railway was made based upon the cost efficiency of the mode in comparison to the horse-drawn alternative. With the expansion into cotton transportation, the railway expanded its footprint on the supply chain from raw material sourcing to delivery to manufacturing, and with the move into mail distribution the railway

TABLE 2.1 Impact of the innovation on the supply chain and its applicability today

	Plan	Source	Make	Deliver
George Stephenson	The railway enabled more timely, more reliable, and faster transportation for supplies and products from and to greater markets.	The origin of the railway was in coal mining and the cost-efficient sourcing of a key source of fuel in the Industrial Revolution.	The transportation of cotton expanded the service into manufacturing.	By delivering mail and produce from farms, the railway expanded timely access to new markets and affordable access for consumers. Railways also connected to other modes of transportation such as ocean shipping. The large market for public transportation drove yields on investment in railways.
Today	The railway is an alternative to growing shortage of truck drivers in the US and congested roads in Europe.			Railways are part of a larger set of transportation options with the opportunity to positively impact sustainability performance in the supply chain.

established its impact not just on cost efficiency but also on more timely and reliable distribution. This in turn enabled greater market access for the perishable produce of farmers and improved affordable product availability for consumers.

Today, as an alternative to air and road transportation, rail produces fewer CO_2 emissions and, as a result, can make a positive contribution to companies' efforts to improve the sustainability of the supply chain. In addition, shifting more transportation volume to railways can reduce the reliance on truck drivers, who often are in short supply in the United States, and on the use of increasingly congested roads in Europe.

What's Next

As we progress into the fifth Industrial Revolution, the spirit of George Stephenson's work remains valid and deserves further study.

Consider the involvement of a diverse ecosystem of partners, investors, suppliers, and legislators. This very much applies to how companies are experimenting with new technologies and how software is being developed. Blue Yonder, for example, uses an open development platform for its supply chain software, and many consumer products companies, including Procter & Gamble, use open innovation sourcing to accelerate their product roadmap (van Hoek et al. 2020).

The gradual nature of change and the importance of self-education and persistent, continued discovery and learning hold great relevance today. Stephenson was self-educated and he was illiterate until the age of eighteen. A lot of the work that carried Stephenson up the ladder of engineers in mining was based upon discovery and experimentation instead of a reliance on abstract science and an existing body of academic theory.

The dynamic nature of modern supply chains and industry 4.0 not only calls for lifelong learning (WEF 2018); it also requires the discovery and exploration of newer technologies. Relying on the existing body of scientific knowledge will not suffice. We may need many George Stephenson's in the future who do not overrely on scientific theory but who experiment from one project to the next with hands-on application and implementation.

The interconnectivity between modes of transportation is found in the interconnectivity of industry 4.0 technologies. Blockchains, for example, may use data feeds from RFID tags, bar codes, and sensory data. The fact that proof of concept of a technology does not mean effective adoption of a technology, as seen with the locomotive, also rings true for industry 4.0 technologies, including blockchain. Blockchain is a proven technology, but its adoption is limited today (van Hoek 2019). And while there is much talk of transformative technology, it appears that the careful consideration and gradual adoption of these technologies, mirroring that of the railway technology, deserves further focus.

The same is true for the need for standard setting around those technologies and litigation of their use. Standard setting may ensure the ability to connect not only within technology (rail to rail) but also between technologies (sensor to blockchain, for example). And while nineteenth-century railway projects needed acts of Parliament, governments today debate social media's influence on elections, data security, and cyber risks. Perhaps a few legislative acts around industry 4.0 may be relevant.

Also, many new roles and professions are being created in industry 4.0 (WEF 2018), just as Stephenson did in the railway industry. Data analysts, for instance, could be the new navvies.

Finally, the railway was initially justified as a cost-efficient alternative to horse-drawn carts, but its full contribution to supply chain objectives was also found in reliability, speed, and market access. Many technology considerations today prominently focus on cost benefits. Robots, for example, can be less expensive and more productive than human workers. But this is only part of the benefit. Robotics also can provide greater supply chain transparency and more timely and accurate data for decision making. As a result, the contributions of supply chain innovation will continue to multiply if we continue to learn, discover, and advance real world practice.

George Stephenson Timeline

1530s—Wooden boards are laid on the ground in Germany to make it easier for horses to pull truckloads of cargo from mines.

1700s—Wooden rails are used in mining operations; horses provide the power.

1712—Thomas Newcomen produces the first steam pump.

1770s—The mining industry advances from wooden to cast-iron rails.

1782—James Watt perfects a steam engine that can turn wheels.

1801—Richard Trevithick builds the first locomotive; it's powered by a steam engine and runs on unpaved roads rather than tracks.

1804—Trevithick builds a second locomotive, this one designed to run on rails, but the rails of that time are unable to handle the machine's weight and he later abandons the idea.

1810—Stephenson, at the age of twenty-nine, successfully leads a last-ditch effort to modify a faulty steam engine that pumped water out of the Killingworth High Pit coal mine, earning him a promotion from brakeman to engineman. By 1812 he is promoted to engine-wright, which puts him in charge of all the colliery's machinery.

1812—John Blenkinsop builds the first commercially successful loco-motive and track in a mine near Leeds, England.

May 23, 1822—Stephenson's crews lay the first tracks for the nine-mile railway from Darlington to Stockton; the plans originally called for a horse-drawn train, but Stephenson switches to steam power because he is convinced it will be faster and more cost efficient.

May 1824—Stephenson also is commissioned as engineer for the Liverpool to Manchester line, which would become the first intercity railway and the first to use two-way tracks and signaling.

September 27, 1825—The Darlington-Stockton line opens with a steam-powered locomotive pulling ninety tons of cargo and people at top speeds of fifteen miles per hour. Stephenson engineered the route, locomotive, cart, tracks (using malleable iron), and junc-tions (using cast iron), and worked with investors to get the project privately financed, litigated through Parliament, and into operation. It is the first public railway with a steam locomotive for coal trans-portation and the general public.

References

Bailey, M. R. 1999. "Decision-Making Processes in the Manufacturing Sector: The Independent Locomotive Industry in the 19th Century." PhD thesis, University of York.

Bailey, M. R., ed. 2003. *Robert Stephenson, the Eminent Engineer.* Farnham, UK: Ashgate.

Davies, H. 1975. *A Biographical Study of the Father of Railways George Stephenson.* London: Weidenfeld and Nicolson.

Hoek, R. van. 2019. "Exploring Blockchain Implementation in the Supply Chain: Learning from Pioneers and RFID Research." *International Journal of Operations & Production Management* 39, no. 6/7/8, 829–859.

Hoek, R. van, M. Johnson, J. Godsell, and A. Birtwistle. 2010. "Changing Chains: Three Case Studies of the Change Management Needed to Reconfigure European Supply Chains." *International Journal of Logistics Management* 21, no. 2, 230–250.

Hoek, R. van, V. Sankararaman, T. Udesen, T. Geurts, and D. G. Palumbo-Miele. 2020. "Where We Are Heading and the Research That Can Help Us Get There—Executive Perspectives on the Anniversary of the Journal of Purchasing and Supply Management." *Journal of Purchasing and Supply Management* 26, no. 3, 100621.

Officer, Lawrence H. 2024. "Dollar-Pound Exchange Rate from 1791." MeasuringWorth. All conversion rates in this chapter to current US dollars are from https://www.measuringworth.com/datasets/exchangepound/result.php.

Ross, D. 2010. *George and Robert Stephenson. A Passion for Success.* Strout, UK: The History Press.

Smiles, S. 1857. *The Life of George Stephenson.* London: John Murray.

Smiles, S. 1868. *The Life of George Stephenson and of His Son Robert Stephenson, Comprising Also a History of the Invention and Introduction of the Railway Locomotive.* London: John Murray. Available publicly on Google Books. https://www.google.com/books/edition/The_Life_of_George_Stephenson_and_of_His/FKRcAAAAcAAJ?hl=en&gbpv=1&dq=The+Life+of+George+Stephenson+and+of+Son+Robert+Stephenson,+Comprising+Also+a+History+of+the+Invention+and+Introduction+of+the+Railway+Locomotive&p.

WEF (World Economic Forum). 2018. *The Future of Jobs Report.* Geneva: World Economic Forum.

Wood, N. 1825. *A Practical Treatise on Rail-roads.* London: Knight and Lacey.

Henry Ford

Birth: July 30, 1863
Died: April 7, 1947 (age 83)
Company: Ford Motor Company
Hall of Fame Induction: 2016
Key Supply Chain Innovation: Pioneer of assembly line production

The path to innovation almost always includes two things: unique ideas that solve a problem and obstacles that stand in the way of giving those ideas a life. Many wonderful ideas end up hitting the obstacles and bouncing quietly back into oblivion. True innovators find a way to take their ideas around, under, over, or—in at least one instance involving Henry Ford—right through the impediments.

In June 1896, three months after watching Charles Brady King successfully drive a gas-powered vehicle down the cobblestone streets of Detroit, Ford finally was ready to test-drive his own version of the horseless carriage—the "Quadricycle Runabout." But when it was time to roll the vehicle out of the coal shed where it was built, he realized there was a significant problem: the car was too big to fit through the shed's doorway.

Here's how Steven Watts, author of *The People's Tycoon,* described Ford's response to that particular obstacle: "He grabbed an ax and doubled the opening by knocking out some bricks" (2009).

Freed from the confines of the shed, Ford began the maiden voyage and soon encountered another obstacle. A spring failed, causing the engine to stop. Fortunately, replacing the spring was much easier than knocking out bricks in a wall, so it didn't take long for him to get rolling again.

When he returned to the shed, which belonged to the landlord of the apartment he was renting, Ford repaired the walls and went off to his day job with the Edison Illuminating Company.

It was neither the first nor the last time Ford found a way to overcome obstacles that stood between him and the life of his ideas. But many historians consider it the breakthrough day for the inventor, who was thirty-three years old at the time and struggling to support his young family while also funding his inventions. If nothing else, it typified the find-a-way attitude that fueled much of Ford's future success. "Obstacles are those frightful things you see when you take your eyes off the goals," Ford would later say (Henry Ford Museum, n.d., "What If?").

Ford, one of the three inaugural inductees into the CSCMP Supply Chain Hall of Fame when it was launched in 2016, was awarded his first patent (for a carburetor) in 1898, and a year later he had raised enough money from investors to pursue automaking full time. He founded Ford Motor Company in 1903 and introduced the Model T—the first car affordable to the masses—in 1908.

Ford's greatest contribution to supply chain innovation is easily summed up in two words: assembly line. But in reality, helping to create the first significant assembly line in manufacturing was just one part of Ford's extraordinary involvement in reshaping how products are made and moved to market. As Ford's career in manufacturing progressed, he helped design a comprehensive supply chain ranging from source to delivery that impacted later generations of Hall of Famers and innovators such as Michael Dell, Peter Drucker, and Sam Walton.

There are several lesser-known aspects to his contributions to supply chain design, including that he provided the foundation for just-in-time and waste elimination, more commonly attributed to lean manufacturing. Perhaps most importantly, Ford's innovations remain foundational to modern business, albeit in advanced forms that, with ongoing development and research, continue to see improvements on his original ideas.

Everything Moves

While Ford gets credit for the moving assembly line, he did not invent it. In the 1870s, slaughterhouses in Chicago and Cincinnati used moving deassembly lines, suspending carcasses on monorail trolleys that moved the meat from stationary worker to stationary worker for another step in the butchering process. Other industries—flour mills, breweries, canneries, and industrial bakers, for instance—also used some type of continuous-flow production methods (Hounshell 1984). So early versions were up and running in different industries and parts of America before Ford ever considered the concept.

In July 1908, production manager Charles Sorensen and a few workers began spending their Sundays experimenting with a moving assembly line on the third floor of Ford's Piquette Avenue Plant. Rather than keeping the chassis in one place and bringing the various components to assemble the car, Sorensen moved the chassis from one end of the plant toward the other, starting with a frame, adding axles and wheels, and then moving it past the stockroom. A few weeks later, they used the method to assemble a Model N (Hyde 2005).

"We did this simply by putting the frame on skids, hitching a towrope to the front end and pulling the frame along until axles and wheels were put on," Sorensen said. "Then we rolled the chassis along in notches to prove what could be done" (Hyde 2005).

Ford watched the first demonstration and encouraged the experiments, but most of his focus in 1908 was on the debut of the Model T, the model that made the automobile industry. By 1910, Ford had moved most of its operations to its expansive new Highland Park Plant, and in April 1913 his team introduced the assembly-line approach. It wasn't just a part of the production process—it defined the production process. An entire supply chain was built around it over the years that followed. This technique decreased the time it took to build a car from twelve hours to two and a half and thereby lowered the cost of the Model T from $850 in 1908 to $310 by 1926 (Biography.com 2019).

The flow—or what Ford called "everything moves"—eventually expanded from something that happened within a particular process to something that went on between departments within a factory to something that continued between factories in different locations.

Ford's first assembly line, however, only involved the production of the flywheel magneto. The first chassis were assembled on the line a few months later, in August 1913.

"With one workman doing a complete job he could turn out from 35 to 40 pieces in a nine-hour day, or about 20 minutes to an assembly," Ford said. "What he did alone was then spread into 29 operations; that cut down the assembly time to 13 min., 10 sec. Then we raised the height of the line eight inches—this was in 1914—and cut the time to seven minutes. Further experimenting with the speed that the work should move at cut the time down to five minutes. . . . That line established the efficiency of the method of assembly and we now use it everywhere" (*Automotive Manufacturer* 1922).

The focus of the assembly line was on productivity, automation, and tooling, and on organizing the work around labor, not the other way around. "The first step forward in assembly came when we began taking the work to the men instead of the men to the work," Ford said (1924).

Here's how he outlined the principles of assembly:

(1) Place the tools and the men in the sequence of the operation so that each component part shall travel the least possible distance while in the process of finishing.

(2) Use work slides or some form of carrier so that when a workman completes his operation, he drops the part always in the same place—which place must always be the most convenient place to his hand.

(3) Use sliding assembling lines by which the parts to be assembled are delivered at convenient distance (Ford 1924).

In addition to the concept of the product flowing to the workers and shop floor optimization, the other keys to Ford's innovation involved the division of labor, specialized machine design, and metal stamping rather than casting (Hounshell 1984).

David Nye (2013) identified three additional key elements of the production system: (1) the use of interchangeable parts that could fit smoothly together without the need for any last-minute sanding, filling, or polishing; (2) electrification of machines so there were no performance variations and works in progress ran a lower risk of spoiling due to lack of heat; and (3) arrangement of machines not by type but instead according to the sequence of the work.

The division of labor and the departmentalization of work created a system in which an individual worker performed one discrete task rather than making a part or product from start to finish. This enabled standardization and productivity, leading to shortened production times and the opportunity to scale production to higher volumes.

The subdivision of labor also made it possible for almost everybody to be employed in the factory (Ford 1924), which significantly decreased unemployment in the region. The economies of scale and reduced production times lowered product costs (see Table 3.1), which enabled the company to sell at lower prices. That resulted in perhaps the biggest impact of the innovation: it made a high-quality product available to the masses and led to the motorization of modern society.

Bottomland to Integrated Supply Chain

In 1915, Ford began buying property along the Rouge River, thinking that perhaps he might turn it into a bird sanctuary. Instead, the US government called on Ford when it needed boats during World War I, and in 1917 the three-story "Building B" went up with the purpose of

TABLE 3.1 Automotive production of the Ford Motor Company, 1908–1917

Years	Production volume	Change in production volume (%)	Price in $	Change of price (%)
1908–1909	10,660		950	
1909–1910	19,051	79	780	−18
1910–1911	34,070	79	690	−12
1911–1912	76,150	124	600	−13
1912–1913	181,951	139	550	−8
1913–1914	264,972	46	490	−11
1914–1915	283,161	7	440	−10
1915–1916	534,108	89	360	−18
1916–1917	785,433	47	360	0

Source: Casey 2008

manufacturing warships that would combat German submarines (Henry Ford Museum, n.d., "Henry Ford's Rouge").

The war ended before these "Eagle Boats" saw action, but the Rouge River Plant (Figure 3.1) would have a lasting impact on Ford's company and on supply chain history. The boat-building project allowed Ford to widen the Rouge River, which allowed ore boats to use the waterway. Before long, boats brought iron ore, coal, and limestone directly to the factory, where everything from engine blocks to exhaust manifolds were made at what once was the largest foundry on earth (Henry Ford Museum, n.d., "Henry Ford's Rouge").

Virtually every component of the Model T was produced at the Rouge and then assembled at Highland Park, but in 1921 the Rouge began mass-producing tractors for farming. By then, Ford also had built a power plant on the river property that provided electricity for the facility and about a third of what was needed at Highland Park. And in 1927, when the Model A was made at the Rouge, the plant became known for its "ore to assembly" automobiles (Henry Ford Museum, n.d., "Henry Ford's Rouge").

Ford never had fewer than six thousand suppliers that served the Rouge, so he never achieved his vision of total self-sufficiency. But the company, according to the Henry Ford Museum (n.d., "Henry Ford's Rouge"), "once owned 700,000 acres of forest, iron mines and limestone quarries in northern Michigan, Minnesota, and Wisconsin. Ford mines covered thousands

FIGURE 3.1 The Rouge River Plant in 1940

Source: The Henry Ford Museum

of acres of coal-rich land in Kentucky, West Virginia, and Pennsylvania. Ford even purchased and operated a rubber plantation in Brazil."

Ford's subdivision of labor and departmentalization of work led to the creation of a factory that looked like a city with many subassemblies feeding into the final assembly of finished cars. By 1940 the Rouge plant produced a complete car, from raw materials, in twenty-eight hours (see Figure 3.1). There were 7,882 different jobs in the factory (Nye 2013).

The term "supply chain management" didn't find its way into the business lexicon until much later, but researcher Albert Corominas (2013) points out that Ford factored in transportation considerations when picking plant locations, saw factories as interconnected, and designed a system for producing and distributing cars as a whole, arguably making him the first modern supply chain manager long before the term was coined.

Railroads and ore ships became an integrated part of the system to help control transportation inventories while reducing manufacturing cycles from twenty-eight days to three days (Wilson 1995). In 1926, Ford had a fully integrated supply chain with stock visibility throughout and a balanced production cycle that shortened the time from the mine to the finished product in the freight car to eighty-one hours—something many organizations today would still envy (Morgan 2004).

Ford's Principles Exemplified

As one of the first, if not the first, modern supply chain managers, Ford deserves credit for several key supply chain management and leadership principles.

Making new customer value and service possible. The fundamental reason for the success of the Ford production system is that he made quality products available at price points previously unthinkable. The supply chain innovations directly contributed to new customer options and ultimately to changing society and the economy by making affordable cars available to everyone.

"I will build a motor car for the great multitude," Ford said. "It will be large enough for the family but small enough for the individual to run and care for. It will be constructed of the best materials, by the best men to be hired, after the simplest design that modern engineering can devise. But it will be so low in price that no man making a good salary will be unable to own one—and enjoy with his family the blessings of pleasure of God's great open spaces" (Casey 2008).

Approaching manufacturing as a wholistic flow. Ford was among the first to proactively consider each stage in the supply chain, from raw materials to the final product being shipped.

"Henry Ford pointed out some fundamental conditions required for the well-functioning of the marketing channel," noted Goran Svensson (2002), a professor at the Oslo School of Management. "His thoughts of almost a century ago are nowadays an essential part of supply chain management."

Using continuous improvement to drive everyday progress. "Hardly a week passes without some improvement being made somewhere in machine or process," Ford (1924) wrote, "and sometimes this is made in defiance of what is called 'the best shop practice.'" To illustrate the effect: in 1909 it took twelve hours to assemble a car; in 1914 it took ninety-three minutes (Nye 2013).

Using analytics to drive improvements. By the early 1920s, Ford had a time studies department with sixty staff members who studied and designed tasks for operators. This was key not only to higher productivity, but also to ensuring continuous flow of the assembly line (Nye 2013).

Using technology and tooling as key enablers. From the electrification of production to investing in equipment and tools on an ongoing basis, the innovations in the production system were fueled by technology and automation that improved productivity and quality. Note, however, that the key focus of improvements was on enabling productivity in human work; technology served principally as an enabler.

"Machines were devised not to do a man out of a job," Ford said in a 1930 interview with the *Detroit Free Press*, "but to take the heavy labor from man's back and place it on the broad back of the machine" (Henry Ford Museum, n.d., "Henry Ford Quotations").

Expanding the vision for business impact. Supply chains can help make the world a better place. Ford's innovations in business and society did not just create new manufacturing processes and capabilities. They also created the potential of full employment in the economy and made motorized transportation accessible for the masses. Ford certainly had his ideological flaws, but he fundamentally believed leaders had a responsibility to make the world better.

In his words:

"A big business never becomes big by being a narrow society looking after only the interests of its organization and stockholders" (Henry Ford Museum, n.d., "Henry Ford Quotations").

"The only true test of values, either of men or of things, is that of their ability to make the world a better place in which to live" (Henry Ford Museum, n.d., "Henry Ford Quotations").

"The great need of the world has always been for leaders. With more leaders we could have more industry. More industry, more employment and comfort for all" (Henry Ford Museum, n.d., "Henry Ford Quotations").

FIGURE 3.2 Ford flexible assembly-line production 1913–1915

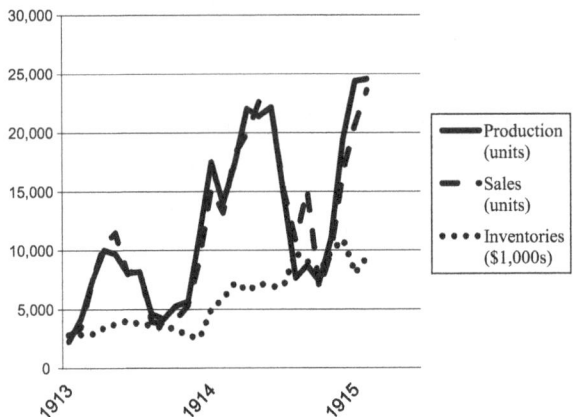

Source: Wilson, 2018

In addition to the supply chain lessons that are routinely attributed to Ford, there are others for which he typically gets little or no credit but where his impact is clearly evident. At least two areas of supply chain capability can be found in the Ford production system, for instance, that normally are not associated with Ford.

Flexibility and demand responsiveness. The focus on productivity and production control in the Ford production system is often mistaken for a lack of flexibility and attention to demand levels. Figure 3.2, however, illustrates how production was closely matched to highly variable sales, while minimizing inventories (Wilson 2018).

The Ford factories had multiple production lines, some of which could be temporarily closed or reopened depending on demand volumes. And Ford saw lines as individual production systems, as well as considering them globally within the supply chain overall.

Just-in-time and lean production. Taiichi Ohno, the inventor of just-in-time and lean production, indicated that he learned from Ford and built on those foundations to develop lean manufacturing (Sutherland and Bennett 2007; Wilson 1995).

Ford focused on quality, inventory reduction, and continuously flowing parts and subassemblies through the process, leading to shorter and shorter cycle times and providing fodder for the post–World War I development of the lean production systems in Japan (Stonebraker and Afifi 2004). Work-in-progress inventory, for example, was kept to a minimum.

"We found in buying material that it is not worthwhile to buy for other than immediate needs," Ford (1924) said. "We buy only enough to fit into the plan of production, taking into consideration the state of transportation at the time. If transportation were perfect and an even flow of materials could be assured, it would not be necessary to carry any stock whatsoever."

Links to Other Supply Chain Innovators

Just as Ford built upon the ideas of other industries and collaborators, so did his work provide an impetus for further innovation and development. In fact, there are several connections to other Hall of Fame inductees and leading supply chain innovators.

Sam Walton built his retail formula around using efficient logistics and scale to achieve low-cost offerings to consumers. In many respects, this is an application of Ford's approach but in the retail space, and one that equally hinges on the interplay among logistics, scale, and customers. Walton advanced Ford's innovations because everyday low pricing in supercenters also brought growing levels of product variety and unmatched levels of reliable availability (Mason-Jones and Towill 1998).

Michael Dell's business model of a direct-to-consumer mass customized product with dynamic pricing adjusting for product availability builds upon the manufacturing approach that departmentalizes and cuts the product into subassemblies that feed into final assembly. Assembling subassemblies to order, however, was an advancement that, coupled with different module options, enabled customization (within limits) at mass scale. Introducing dynamic pricing created a mechanism to further the alignment of production to customer demand. Dell did this not only by using flexible manufacturing and reducing speculative inventory, but also by influencing demand with discounting, specials, and other pricing strategies.

Peter Drucker's work on outsourcing was in many respects inspired by Ford. The vertical integration achieved by Ford for the purpose of efficiency and flow control, Drucker reasoned, might be achievable in a similar supply chain setting, without requiring ownership. The progression from control by ownership to cooperating to competing led to the more complex, multitier supply chains we are accustomed to today.

Eliyahu Goldratt's focus on resolving constraints in a system to establish flow can be very much linked back to Ford's "everything flows" philosophy. Goldratt advanced Ford's insight by applying the concepts more broadly to business, managerial, and operational processes, not just in manufacturing and logistics.

Today's Relevance

The continuing impact of Ford's innovations on supply chain managers can be viewed in two main categories: leadership and process.

When it comes to leadership, for instance, here are five best practices from Ford that remain highly relevant for today's supply chain leaders:

1. **Making failure safe because failure is part of innovation and continuous improvement.**
   "The factory," Ford (1924) noted, "keeps no record of experiments. . . . If you keep on recording all of your failures you will shortly have a list showing that there is nothing left for you to try—whereas it by no means follows because one man has failed in a certain method that another man will not succeed."

2. **Hard work and humility are a service to others.**
   When Ford opened his museum on American innovation, he devoted it to Thomas Edison, whose company he had worked for before starting the Ford Motor Company. It was not named for Ford until after he died. This, coupled with a focus on hard work and continuous improvement, exemplifies the mentality of many supply chain managers today.

   "Whether a man chooses employment or a business of his own for his career," Ford said, "his first step is the same; he must go to work and learn his job. . . . Whatever your goal in life, the beginning is knowledge and experience—or, briefly, work" (Henry Ford Museum, n.d., "Henry Ford Quotes").

3. **Leaders can transfer between industries and exchange best practices.**

   Ford started his career with Edison and credited him as an inspiration and mentor. He also said at one point that aviation was the great industrial need in America. Studying the disassembly line in the meat industry was another of many examples of how Ford learned across industry boundaries and exported inventions and insights.

4. **Success involves collaboration.**

   Ford did not invent the assembly line or the production system on his own but collaborated with other leaders and across teams. He supported and invested in experimentation and exploration and engaged in discussions with his staff, and collectively they invented the production systems (Nye 2013).

5. **The need for lifelong learning for all.**

   Ford recognized, as do the best modern leaders, that ongoing education is essential to continued success. A philosophy of lifelong learning shaped not only his leadership but the culture of his company.

   "Education is not just preparation for life, but part of life itself—a continuous art," Ford said in one interview (Henry Ford Museum, n.d., "Henry Ford Quotations").

The vertical integration practiced by Ford is not feasible in modern markets because of the capital investment needed and the complex organization that it requires. And, indeed, the variation and speed of innovation today have given rise to expansive supply chains and transportation systems around the world that run across, not within, a company. But Ford's innovations still play a key role in the four main stages of a supply chain—plan, source, make, and deliver (Table 3.2).

The "plan" stage today increasingly needs to allow for the agility and variety demanded by modern markets, coupled with efficiency and affordability. As a result, the focus on analytics, so crucial in Ford's efforts to optimize flow and productivity, is shifting toward improving responsiveness and planning accuracies.

TABLE 3.2 Impact of the innovation on the supply chain and its applicability today

	Plan	Source	Make	Deliver
Henry Ford	Optimization of labor productivity while monitoring demand to align manufacturing with demand and keep speculative inventory to a minimum.	Vertically integrated supply operations, driven by the desire to optimize labor productivity to reduce cost.	Primary focus—flow optimization, automation, and division of labor to boost productivity and enable scaling of volume and reduction of pricing.	Transportation between stages of the production process and from the plant to the customer, part of the focus on flow efficiency.
Today	Growing focus on agility and variety, not just affordability, as well as the use of analytics to improve planning accuracy.	Collaborate with suppliers to reduce the need to vertically integrate and as a result reduce investment needed and grow innovation potential.	Robotics enables a migration from optimizing around men to doing so with equipment, allowing for greater variety, at speed.	Need to optimize not just for efficiency but also for variety and speed to the consumer.

In manufacturing, the focus on automation to enable labor is migrating away from optimization around labor toward a focus on deploying robotics and automation to repurpose labor. Automation is focused less on productivity enhancement and more on freeing up labor for higher-value-added tasks and reducing the need for labor in basic processes. Robotics can also enable more speed in operational processes while increasing flexibility to drive variety. Consider self-driving robots that move parts from storage to shipment, for example; these are not limited to one simple task as in the ideal of the Ford division of labor.

In delivery, finally, the Ford production system included an innovative focus on inbound and in-plant logistics. And delivery to the customer was part of these considerations; the supply chain focus was not limited to materials management. For example, as Figure 3.3 illustrates, if a Model T leaving the assembly lines at Ford's Highland Park Plant was going to be shipped by rail, it was not fully assembled; car bodies and

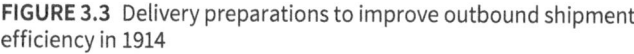

FIGURE 3.3 Delivery preparations to improve outbound shipment efficiency in 1914

Source: The Henry Ford Museum

wheels would be removed and packed separately to conserve freight car space. The remaining assembly took place at branch plants closer to the vehicles' destination. Today, a focus on outbound delivery would need to allow for mass customization and much higher expectations around fast and timely delivery.

High-quality, affordable products have become a consumer expectation, and variety of choice and speed of response are increasingly added to those expectations. The response to that progression in supply chain management has been to turn to suppliers around the world for capabilities, resources, and innovation potential.

The move away from vertical integration has led to the creation of more complex, global and local multiple-tier supply chains that are in great need of technology and supplier relationship management to prevent the problems solved by the Ford system—the bullwhip effect, aligning production with demand, and reducing speculative inventory—

while continuously improving and educating staff on improvements and innovations.

As a result, a lot of the supply chain lessons and approaches that Henry Ford's system and leadership exemplified (such as a focus on education and collaboration) are still very relevant and may still further inspire key progress in capability development.

What's Next

Because of the foundation the Ford production system provided, as well as its continuing relevance to modern supply chains, the opportunities to innovate further for the good of future supply chain performance are great. Here are a few ways to build on Ford's supply chain legacy:

1. **The changing role of the human versus the machine.**
   Whereas Ford focused on automation to reduce the workload on humans and to enable productivity, a lot of automation today can dispose of the need for humans. Dark warehouses and factories are becoming options. These advancements, however, do not eliminate the need for humans in the supply chain. In fact, they may take the fundamental premise of Ford to the next level: to not only support operational productivity, but also to empower humans by freeing them to focus on experimentation and innovation.

   Beyond automating the assembly line, automating relationships with supply chain partners and customers could be a key frontier for capability enhancement (Viswanadham 2002). The questions are, where do machines end, where do humans begin, and how do they interact? This is clearly a divide that is in motion, but it may not be a hard divide at all. Just as Ford focused on making tools easily reachable for his frontline workers, so too is there an opportunity to research how modern technologies can be at frontline workers' fingertips for greater supply chain capability, driven by humans and leveraging technology.

2. **Reconsidering the bullwhip effect.**
   Departmentalization and the creation of subassemblies introduce the risk of the bullwhip effect, and this risk has grown

with the departure of a focus on vertical integration. In fact, the risks are growing in today's increasingly complex supply chains that combine very global with partly local operations and that strive for fast delivery of a greater variety of products. As a result, it is relevant to consider where the divide between insourcing and outsourcing needs to fall in different markets and industries.

Ford reduced the risk of the bullwhip effect through vertical integration and product range standardization. Hence, there may be opportunities to nuance the focus on cross–supply chain cooperation and consider selective re-insourcing, if it means we can more reliably manage customer fulfillment.

3. **Making experimentation and innovation safe across companies.**
Reconsidering vertical integration may be less feasible in markets with growing customization, variety, and accelerated innovation cycles. It's worth asking, and researching, how the Ford culture of focusing on experimentation and making failure safe could be expanded across companies in the supply chain that also have direct trading relationships with each other.

4. **The role of lifelong learning and engagement of leaders in industry 4.0.**
The World Economic Forum (2018) suggests that the need for reskilling, upskilling, and lifelong learning is a key implication of the move toward industry 4.0. Ford likely would have said, "Told you so."

Key questions for leaders today include how to create lifelong learning environments, how to make failure safe, and, perhaps most importantly, how to engage as a leader to make those goals a reality. Ford provided a role model for appreciating and personally engaging in education as a leader.

5. **Extending the supply chain canon beyond Henry Ford.**
The many connections between the original supply chain efforts of Ford and several Hall of Famers who came after him make it clear that innovation breeds innovation. It will be interesting, in turn, to explore how leaders of today and tomorrow carry the supply chain canon forward.

Ford once predicted that all families would have a small plane in their backyards, and drone delivery may be making that a reality. What other problem-solving ideas will emerge in the supply chain industry? More importantly, who will take an axe and break down the walls that stand between those ideas and a new reality?

Henry Ford Timeline

1870s—Slaughterhouses in Chicago and Cincinnati begin suspending carcasses on monorail trollies that move the meat between stationary workers for each step in the butchering process.

June 1896—Three months after watching Charles Brady King successfully drive a gas-powered vehicle down the cobblestone streets of Detroit, Ford test-drives his own version of the horseless carriage—the "Quadricycle Runabout."

1898—Ford is awarded his first patent (for a carburetor).

1899—Funded by investors, Ford begins pursuing automaking full time.

June 16, 1903—The Ford Motor Company is formed and begins assembling the Ford Model A at the Ford Mack Avenue Plant, a former wagon manufacturing shop in Detroit, Michigan.

October 1904—Ford Motor Company moves its operations to the Piquette Avenue Plant, a three-story factory with more than 67,000 square feet.

1908—A small group of workers at the Piquette Avenue Plant working in their off hours successfully assemble a Model N using a moving-assembly approach, but the process is not yet incorporated into the company's manufacturing process.

1908—Ford introduces the Model T, considered the first car affordable to the masses.

1910—Ford's Highland Park Plant opens in Detroit, Michigan, and it eventually includes offices, factories, a power plant, and a foundry on 102 acres.

April 1913—Ford and his team begin using a moving assembly line for the production of the flywheel magneto. Eventually, the line expands and parts are added at workstations until a complete car rolls out.

1915—Ford begins buying property along the Rouge River, initially thinking he might turn it into a bird sanctuary.

1917—The Rouge River property becomes home to a factory designed to build "Eagle Boats" for use against German submarines in World War I. The war ends before the boats are deployed, but the factory soon becomes the largest foundry on earth, making everything from engine blocks to exhaust manifolds for assembly into automobiles at Ford's Highland Park facility.

1920s—About sixty workers make up Ford's "time studies department," all tasked with designing more efficient operations.

1927—After mass-producing tractors for farming, the Rouge River Plant begins making the Model A and becomes an "ore to assembly" automobile factory.

1940—The Rouge River Plant is producing a complete car from raw materials in just twenty-eight hours.

References

Biography.com. 2019. "Henry Ford." Updated September 5, 2019. https://www.biography.com/business-leaders/henry-ford.

Casey, R. 2008. *A Centennial History, The Model T.* Baltimore: Johns Hopkins University Press.

Corominas, A. 2013. "Supply Chains: What They Are and the New Problems They Raise." *International Journal of Production Research* 51, no. 23–24, 6828–6835.

Ford, H., and S. Crowther. 1924. *My Life and Work.* London: William Heinemann.

Henry Ford Museum of American Innovation. n.d. "Henry Ford Quotations." https://www.thehenryford.org/collections-and-research/digital-resources/popular-topics/henry-ford-quotes/.

Henry Ford Museum of American Innovation. n.d. "Henry Ford Quotes." henryfordquotes-long.xls, www.thehenryford.org.

Henry Ford Museum of American Innovation. n.d. "Henry Ford's Rouge." https://www.thehenryford.org/visit/ford-rouge-factory-tour/history-and-timeline/fords-rouge/.

Henry Ford Museum of American Innovation. n.d. "What If Henry Ford Never Finished Building His First Automobile?" https://www.thehenryford.org/explore/stories-of-innovation/what-if/henry-ford/.

Hounshell, D. 1984. *From the American System to Mass Production, 1800–1932.* Baltimore: Johns Hopkins University Press.

"How Ford Works Out Its Assembly." 1922. *Automotive Manufacturer* LXIV, no. 6, p. 17.

Hyde, Charles. 2005. "National Historic Landmark Nomination—Ford Piquette Avenue Plant." National Park Service, June. Accessed June 14, 2021. http://www.nps.gov/nhl /find/statelists/mi/FordPiquette.pdf.

Mason-Jones, R., and D. R. Towill. 1998. "Time Compression in the Supply Chain: Information Management Is the Vital Ingredient." *Logistics Information Management* 11, no. 2, 93–104.

Morgan, C. 2004. "Structure, Speed and Salience: Performance Measurement in the Supply Chain." *Business Process Management* 10, no. 5, 522–536.

Nye, D. E. 2013. *America's Assembly Line*. Cambridge, MA: MIT Press.

Stonebraker, P. W., and R. Afifi. 2004. "Towards a Contingency Theory of Supply Chains." *Management Decision* 42, no. 9, 1131–1144.

Sutherland, J. and B. Bennett. 2007. "The Seven Deadly Wastes of Logistics: Applying Toyota Production System Principles to Create Logistics Value." Center for Value Chain Research White Paper 0701, Lehigh University, Bethlehem, Pennsylvania, August.

Svensson, G. (2002), "Supply Chain Management: The Re-integration of Marketing Issues in Logistics Theory and Practice." *European Business Review* 14, no. 6, 426–436.

Viswanadham, N. 2002. "The Past, Present and Future of Supply-chain Automation." *IEEE Robotics & Automation Magazine*, June 2002, 48–56.

Watts, S. 2009. *The People's Tycoon: Henry Ford and the American Century*. (E-book edition), UK: Knopf Doubleday.

Wilson, J. M. 1995. "Henry Ford's Just-in-Time System." *International Journal of Operations & Production Management* 15, no. 12, 59–75.

Wilson, J. M. 2018. "Deconstructing the Reinvention of Operations Management." *Journal of Management History* 24, no. 2, 128–155.

World Economic Forum. 2018. *The Future of Jobs Report*. Geneva: World Economic Forum.

George Laurer

Birth: September 23, 1925
Died: December 5, 2019 (age 94)
Company: IBM
Hall of Fame Induction: 2017
Key Supply Chain Innovation: Developed the coding and pattern used for the Universal Product Code (UPC)

Major advancements in supply chain management often occur in a fashion similar to the way sports teams typically score points. In soccer, for instance, players pass the ball until they get the barrage defenders out of position and there's an opening for a makeable shot on the goal. If ten players do their jobs, then the one with the ball can get it into the goal. Only one player gets credit for the goal, but everyone realizes it took a team effort to score.

When it comes to the development of modern bar code technology, George Laurer scored a game-changing goal that was forty years in the making. It was, to be sure, a team effort, even if some of the key players never were part of Laurer's team. But all of them contributed to a significant innovation in supply chain management—a universally accepted code that was printable, scannable, and readable and that contained key information unique to each product.

A bar code is a machine-readable image encoded with information about the manufacturer and the product. The product's price can be displayed on the register and printed on the receipt, and all the data also feeds into a central computer.

The Universal Product Code (UPC) was a breakthrough technology because its widespread adoption sped customers through checkout lines with fewer pricing errors while collecting valuable data for managing sales and inventory. But that was just the beginning. As Laurer (2012) said, "The UPC code and symbol proved beyond any shadow of a doubt that optical bar codes are viable in industry."

Laurer, an electrical engineer who spent thirty-six years with IBM (International Business Machines), was inducted into the CSCMP Supply Chain Hall of Fame because he came up with the design for the UPC—the bar code and symbol that won near-universal acceptance, first with the grocery industry and then with just about every other industry that makes, ships, or sells a product.

Laurer entered the game a bit late, but that was to his advantage. His fresh take on the challenge was a key to the coding and pattern that he eventually used for the UPC. The development of the technology, however, began decades earlier.

In 1932, for instance, Wallace Flint, a business student at Harvard, wrote a paper proposing an automated checkout system for grocers. Flint had some insights into the need for such a system because his father was a wholesaler. But Flint lacked a few complementary and necessary technologies (the laser and the microchip, for instance), and his vision for readable punch cards and products delivered on flow racks wasn't practical or economically feasible.

In the 1940s, however, Joe Woodland and Bob Silver latched onto the challenge while they were graduate students at the Drexel Institute of Technology. Silver overheard a supermarket manager complaining about the need to get customers through the checkout more efficiently. He mentioned this to Woodland, and the pair began working on a product code that a scanner could read. They realized that with the right information embedded in a code printed on each product, prices could be managed with a computer system rather than by marking or updating products on the shelf, and checkers no longer would have to manually enter data at the register.

Woodland had an epiphany while visiting his grandfather in Miami Beach, Florida. As he ran his fingers through the sand while thinking about the dots and dashes of Morse code, Woodland realized he could make a code using lines of various thickness. He and Silver then developed a bull's-eye–shaped code based on that idea.

They were granted a patent in 1952 for what they called a "classifying apparatus and method," and their nine-page document noted that "one application of the invention is in the so-called supermarket field" (Woodland and Silver 1952). But the prototype machine they developed to read the code was about the size of a standard office desk and it needed a 500-watt incandescent bulb. Without the availability of a far more powerful and concentrated beam of light, their bright idea was too large, expensive, and inefficient for adoption.

It was 1960 before Theodore Maiman developed what he called "Light Amplification by Stimulated Emission of Radiation"—more commonly known as the laser. He envisioned all sorts of uses for an "atomic radio light brighter than the center of the sun," but, as he would later write, "I did not foresee the supermarket check-out scanner or the printer" (Weightman 2015). As it turned out, Maiman's invention was a key piece of advancements in scanning and printing, both of which made the UPC idea more feasible.

Silver and Woodland never incorporated laser technology into their machine. They sold their patent to Philco in 1962 for $15,000, which was all the money the pair ever made for their idea. Silver died in 1963 after a battle with leukemia, but Woodland went to work for IBM and would join Laurer on the UPC project in 1971.

In 1966, meanwhile, an anonymous leader at the Kroger supermarket chain vented a little when putting together a booklet. The last line of the booklet sounded much like the complaint Flint might have heard from his father or Silver might have heard from the store manager: "Just dreaming a little, . . . could an optical scanner read the price and total the sale. . . . Faster service, more productive service is needed desperately" (Weightman 2015).

RCA (Radio Corporation of America) took an interest in that challenge and began working in the late 1960s with Kroger on a solution. RCA did some research, found the patent that had been granted to Woodland and Silver, and bought the patent from Philco. Then RCA commissioned several companies to help create a printable product code and automated checkout stands.

For the idea to take off, however, it needed mass adoption with a universal standard that could be used by both supermarkets and manufacturers.

This was easier envisioned than executed.

In 1969, members of the administrative systems committee of the Grocery Manufacturers of America (GMA) met with their counterparts from the National Association of Food Chains (NAFC) to discuss solutions to the rising costs of grocery sales. But when it came to standards for a workable bar code, they couldn't agree on an approach. The manufacturers wanted an eleven-digit code that would work with labels they already were using, while the retailers argued for a seven-digit code that could be read by simpler, cheaper checkout systems (Harford 2017).

Then in 1970, an industry consortium established an ad hoc committee of ten top executives from H. J. Heinz Co., General Foods Corp., Kroger, General Mills, Associated Foods, Fairmont Foods, Bristol Meyers, A&P, Super Valu Stores, and Madsen Enterprises. They were given the task of setting guidelines for an automated checkout system, and the fact that they were all CEOs, presidents, or chairmen of the board made their work far more effective.

"Executives on this level would have the authority to commit their company without delays required for approvals," Laurer wrote. "The companies represented how to include all facets of the industry, large and small" (Laurer 2012).

The committee solicited proposals from twenty companies (Laurer 2012) and formed a "symbol selection" subcommittee that was charged with creating a standardized approach (Seideman 1993). These committees were the forerunners of the modern GS1, the standards organization that now administers the Global Trade Item Number (GTIN), the identifier encoded in UPC bar codes as well as in advanced data carriers such as two-dimensional (2-D) bar codes and radio frequency identification (RFID) technology.

By 1971, RCA had developed its own bull's-eye product code, which it demonstrated during a grocery industry meeting. An IBM executive watched with interest and IBM soon decided to start its own project, figuring it could design and sell computer systems to manufacturers and retailers. Woodland, now in his fifties, was transferred to North Carolina to help a team that included Laurer.

In the meantime, the industry committee began establishing the criteria for the product codes and their symbols, originally agreeing to use ten digits—five to identify the manufacturer and five to identify the product. For instance, the first five digits on all products made by General Mills are 16000, followed by five digits for the product. So, an 18-ounce box of Cheerios cereal ends up with a UPC of 1600027528, while a 19.5-ounce box of Honey Nut Cheerios has a UPC of 16000123151.

The symbology, meanwhile, needed to be no larger than 1.5 inches square and had to be printed with common label-printing technology. It also needed to be readable from any direction with fewer than 1 in 20,000 undetected errors (GS1, n.d.).

In addition to RCA, a few other companies had proprietary product codes on the market, but none had anything that met all the criteria. Only four were omnidirectional systems, for instance, and only three of those worked with the single-line scanners of that day (Laurer 2012). The bigger problem was that reducing the symbols to the required size made the bars and spaces too small to be printed accurately. Plus, there was always a significant ink smear on the symbols in the direction of the press feed (Laurer 2012).

RCA was considered the front-runner in the code competition. Not only had RCA been working on the project longer than others, but it had successfully installed the first automated checkout stands at a Kroger in Cincinnati on July 3, 1972. And its bull's-eye–style product code was based on the Woodland/Silver model (Weightman 2015).

Originally, IBM intended to endorse the RCA product code. Paul McEnroe, Laurer's supervisor at IBM, assigned Laurer the task of writing a white paper on the RCA code and how IBM could develop technology around it. Laurer was told he had two weeks to craft the paper, during which time McEnroe would be on vacation. On the Monday when McEnroe returned, they would present the paper to IBM executives.

The more Laurer reviewed the circular bull's-eye code, however, the more he was convinced it wouldn't work well with the printers of that time, mainly because it was too prone to smudging. He realized early on that the code and symbol had to be treated as a single entity (Laurer 2012).

"I struggled a day or two but my nature and training would not allow me to support something I did not believe in," Laurer (2012) wrote. "It was obvious to me that (RCA's) approach would never satisfy all the requirements over the long run, even though RCA was demonstrating their system at the time. I simply went against my manager's instruction and set out to design a better system."

Laurer and McEnroe lived across the street from each other, and on the day that McEnroe arrived home from his holiday, he looked up to see Laurer walking over with his arms filled with flipcharts. "Paul, I didn't do what you asked me to," Laurer told his boss. "Instead, I designed a different code" (CSCMP 2017).

In his autobiography, *Engineering Was Fun*, Laurer often describes himself as a "misfit" on a team of hard-to-manage misfits at IBM, and he refers to some of his assignments as "purgatory." So it probably came as no surprise to McEnroe when he learned that Laurer had not followed a directive he had been given.

Laurer showed McEnroe the presentation, walking him through the details of his idea for a rectangular product code that he felt was better than the bull's-eye. With the meeting less than a day away, McEnroe had little option but to go along.

"He said, 'There's nothing I can do about it now,'" Laurer recalled. "'You make the presentation, and if it's not accepted, it's going to be your butt, not mine'" (CSCMP 2017).

The presentation went well, but the executives told Laurer to take his idea to Rochester, Minnesota, and show it to Art Hamburgan and his team of IBM engineers who specialized in optical character reading. "They didn't like it," Laurer said. "They said, 'That's not going to cut it. You can't use it.' So I went back to my desk and I came up with another solution, which was much better than the first one" (CSCMP 2017).

The biggest challenge for the actual symbol, Laurer later said, was keeping it within the size parameters and still producing something that would print clearly and cleanly. From a systems perspective, he said, the challenge was figuring out how to safely incorporate the relatively new laser technologies (IDHistory 2010b).

Laurer worked closely with McEnroe, David Crouse, Herd Baumeister, David Savir, Woodland, and others to fine-tune the modules and character symbols in a product code, as well as the scanner for reading it. For instance, when Laurer suggested an X-pattern to make the code readable from any direction, Baumeister came up with a mirror in the scanner that helped make it work.

Laurer eventually devised a seven-module code with twelve characters that were split into two groups. It included the five digits that identified the manufacturer, the five digits that identified the specific product, a module check digit that was essential to confirming accuracy, and a category code that the committee had requested along the way.

"I reasoned that if I constructed the symbol in two pieces, such that it could read on the same or different passes of the scanning beam and then reassembled in the correct order in the machine, I could reduce the needed area drastically," Laurer explained in a deeply technical appendix in his autobiography. "Such a scheme would allow the addition of the decimal digit for the category value and also another digit to accommodate a module 10 check character all the while allowing even wider minimum bars. Adding the module check character was a natural because it kept the two halves symmetrical—each would have six characters" (2012).

A mistake by the computer was just as likely to overcharge by a million dollars, Laurer noted, as by a few cents, resulting in what his team called the "golden chicken" or "platinum pork" problem. So the "check digit" was as important to consumer confidence as it was to ensuring accuracy.

FIGURE 4.1 An original UPC bar code plate developed by IBM in the 1970s

Source: GS1

"Most people were willing to forgive the sweet young checkout girl for charging $1.98 for a $1.89 item," Laurer wrote, "but would not forgive a machine for charging $99.99 for a pound of chicken even though such a gross error would never go undetected. People just do not forgive machines for making errors" (2012).

Early versions of Lauer's bar code were created manually using individual plates that were assembled in the right order, photographed at a precise distance to make a "film master," affixed to packaging artwork, and printed at scale (Figure 4.1).

Perhaps the biggest internal test of the symbol and system came when the team did a demonstration for B. O. Evans, the head of their division at IBM. "There were many skeptics in IBM," Laurer said, "not the least of whom was B. O. Evans himself" (2012).

After a "flawless demonstration" scanning traditional products in the typical way, the team added a final test just for some flair. "We had our ace softball pitcher pitch bean bag ash trays, with symbols on the bottom, as fast as he could over the scanner," said Laurer. "When each one read correctly, Mr. Evans was convinced" (2012).

Scientists from MIT (Massachusetts Institute of Technology) reviewed IBM's final presentation, along with the symbologies proposed by RCA and five others. They suggested a few modifications, but they ultimately recommended Laurer's option to the selection committee (Weightman 2015).

"One of the things that they required us to change was the font that we used for the printing of the numbers," Laurer said. "We originally used Futura-A as being a rather attractive font. They insisted we changed to OCR-B because they said within five years people would be no longer reading the bars. They would be reading the human readable. So we learned that even the best are not always right" (IDHistory 2010a). On April 3, 1973, the IBM option was officially adopted as the standard UPC, transforming bar codes "from a technological curiosity into a business juggernaut" (Seideman 1993).

Woodland and Laurer often are referenced as cocreators of the UPC, but, as Woodland said, "George Laurer came up with the finest symbology for the supermarket application. He came up with an easy and reliable way to encode and decode UPC data" (IBM, n.d.).

IBM quickly developed a system that included a point-of-sale digital cash register with a checkout scanner that could read the UPC symbol (IBM, n.d.). And on June 26, 1974, a ten-pack of Wrigley's Juicy Fruit gum became the first item marked with a UPC to be scanned in a store (Figure 4.2).

The demonstration took place at the Marsh Supermarket in Troy, Ohio, using checkout equipment provided by National Cash Register. The listed price of the gum was 69 cents, but Marsh's price was 67 cents, and the scanner correctly read the lower price (Harford 2017; Weightman 2015; Smith 2019).

"It is Norman Woodland who is often regarded as the pioneer who invented the first version of the bar code," a statement from GS1 noted in 2019 after Laurer died. "However, it is George Laurer who made the bar code practical to use by industry through low-cost laser and computing technology, and therefore changed the way people live all around the globe" (GS1 2019a).

FIGURE 4.2 A replica of the first product scanned in 1974 is in a display case at the GS1 US headquarters in Ewing Township, New Jersey

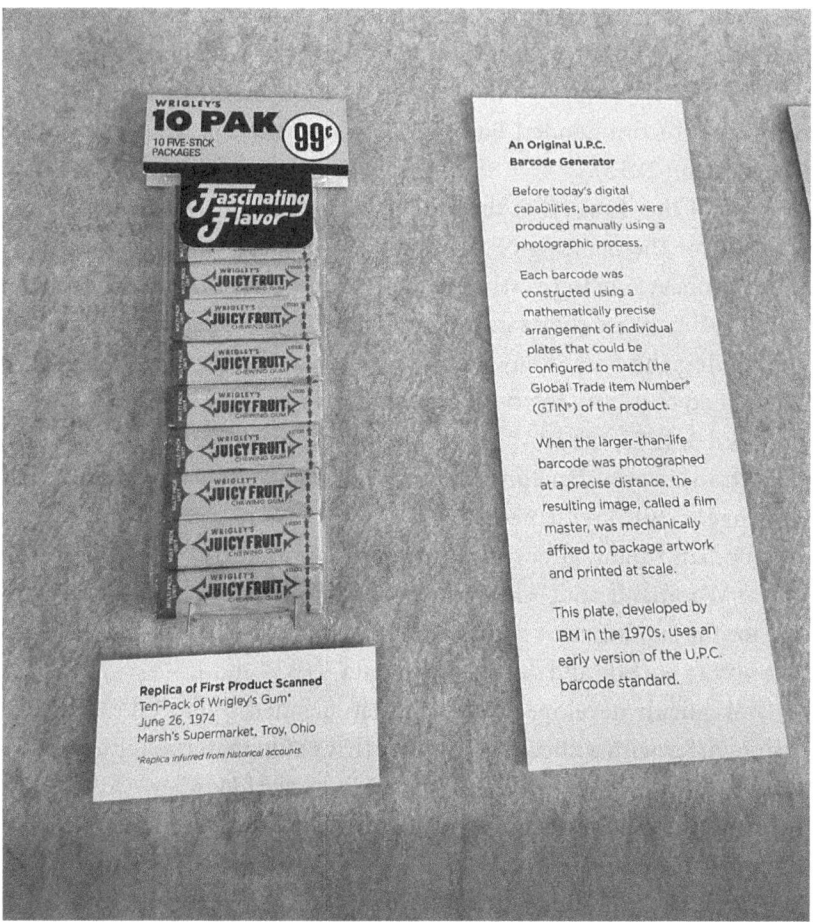

Source: GS1

The Drive for Adoption

The UPC represented a huge business opportunity for the grocery industry. When it was introduced in 1973, for instance, one estimate claimed the average food chain made only eighteen cents on a $30 order and that the industry's after-tax profit margins were at an historic low of 0.6 percent (*Business Week* 1973).

McKinsey & Co., meanwhile, estimated that an electronic scanner and source marking would save the larger supermarkets 1 percent to 1.5 percent of sales before taxes by 1975. A store with $3 million a year in sales, the consultancy estimated, could expect to save $34,700 before taxes. And it estimated a total industry savings of $150 million, after deducting $370 million for installing the new systems (*Business Week* 1973).

None of those estimates included so-called soft savings.

"McKinsey claims that such a system will cut checkout time by half and virtually eliminate the cost of price marking and price changing every item," said a 1973 article in *Business Week* (1973). "It will also reduce store losses caused by error, tighten inventory control, promote faster, more accurate communications from store to warehouse to manufacturer, and furnish in-store evaluation of shelf-allocation changes and pricing policy."

With all those savings as incentives, it would seem likely that quick adoption would follow. And by the end of 1973, the Uniform Grocery Product Code Council (UGPCC) had eight hundred members that accounted for almost 90 percent of nonmeat and non–fresh produce grocery sales. Still, unexpected hurdles slowed the widespread adoption of the bar codes and scanners (Stokel-Walker 2019).

Retailers didn't want to invest in scanner equipment until manufacturers began putting the approved UPC symbols on their products. And the manufacturers didn't want to put the symbols on products until retailers had scanners to read them. "There was the chicken and the egg problem," said Laurer (Stokel-Walker 2019).

IBM's sales team set up a series of briefings in Raleigh, North Carolina, where they explained the UPC and demonstrated it for grocers and for manufacturers, and both Woodland and Laurer often delivered parts of the presentation. Woodland also traveled to association meetings and other events to help explain how the bar code technology worked.

Getting the industry leaders on board, however, was just one part of the process. Fearful that they might lose their jobs, many cashiers opposed the bar codes. And shoppers were far more forgiving of human error, as Laurer noted, than an error by a faceless computer system. They were concerned that mistakes by the technology would cost them money on their weekly grocery bills, and it took some time for them to get used to the new approach to labeling.

"Shoppers had a hard time making the change from not having the item priced on the shelf," Laurer said. "But we found that after a while they changed and nobody even remembers when we used to have to mark the top of the can with the price" (IDHistory 2010a).

And then there were the conspiracy theories, primarily the one the equated the UPC with the apocalyptic mark of the beast referenced in chapter 13 of the book of Revelation in the Bible. The chapter foretells of a force that will require "all people, great and small, rich and poor, free and slave, to receive a mark on their right hands or on their foreheads, so that they could not buy or sell unless they had the mark, which is the name of the beast or the number of its name" (Rev. 13:16–17). It then calculates that the number of the beast is 666. Every coincidental association with the number six was used by some conspiracy theorists to push the idea that the UPC was a tool of Satan that would soon migrate from cola cans to the hands and foreheads of shoppers. "All of this is pure bunk," Laurer said in a 2012 interview, "and is no more important than the fact that my first, middle, and last name all have six letters" (Metz 2012).

Eventually, skeptics, critics, and conspiracists all gave way to the value the UPC added to businesses' operations and to the everyday lives of consumers. In 1978, fewer than 1 percent of grocery stores in the United States had scanners, but that figure rose to 10 percent in 1981, 33 percent by 1984, and more than 60 percent by 1993 (Seideman 1993).

Laurer, meanwhile, updated the UPC to add a digit for foreign countries (the EAN-13 symbol), which allowed the technology to spread globally. And he designed two- and five-digit trailer versions of the UPC for use by publishers, one of many modifications that would take the technology to other industries.

After Laurer retired in June 1987, he and his wife, Marilyn, regularly traveled across North America in their motor home. When they stopped for fuel or other supplies, Marilyn often proudly told the cashiers about her husband's role in the bar codes they were scanning.

"Most of the time people had one of three reactions," Laurer would say. "One was, 'You must be very rich'; another was, 'I don't believe it'; and the third was, 'Gee, didn't we always have bar codes?'" (Stokel-Walker 2019).

Laurer's Principles Exemplified

Laurer's breakthrough innovation provides several important reminders about what it takes to advance the supply chain management industry.

Innovation takes time and teamwork. The bar code concept, as we already noted, developed much like many other supply chain innovations—as a process that took the time and ideas and efforts of several different players.

It not only took the iterative advancements by multiple engineers, especially Woodland, to set the stage for Laurer's efforts; another key factor was the advancement of outside technologies that were needed to make the UPC useful. The original equipment that read a product bar code, for instance, was bulky, inefficient, and expensive. It took advancements outside the industry, primarily the development of the laser, to give this innovation a boast.

Industry collaborations speed up adoption. One of the great impediments to innovation is a territorial attitude by the players throughout an industry. In 1969, leaders from the GMA met with leaders from the NAFC, and both groups realized they needed to work together and make some sacrifices to create change for the greater good.

The next year, an industry consortium established an ad hoc committee composed of senior executives who set the guidelines for developing a universal product code. The consortium guaranteed economies of scale, enabling a drop in costs and ensuring interoperability of the technology from the start.

IBM also recognized that its business would win if the industry won, which is why it never tried to monetize the UPC technology. "IBM made no attempt to patent or otherwise protect the symbol and code because we wanted nothing to deter the use, or slow the implementation, of the UPC symbol," Laurer said. "We gave it to the industry" (2012).

Bill Selmeier, who worked in sales and marketing for IBM and led the team that helped "spread the bar code," pointed out that IBM also took a lead role in marketing the innovation, selling the idea and its benefits before the infrastructure was in place to make it work. In *Spreading the Barcode*, his book on his experience, Selmeier wrote, "Because IBM pushed not only themselves, but worked to sell the whole industry, retailers, grocery manufacturers, and the printing and packaging companies, the U.P.C. Symbol technology became part of the infrastructure and was so successful there has not been a technology sufficiently more productive to replace it even into the 21st century" (2009).

Cost saving and consumer value go hand in hand. Leaders in the retail food industry fell in love with the idea of a scannable product code primarily because it promised efficiencies in their checkout processes that would result in cost savings.

As with many other supply chain innovations, however, it not only saved manufacturers and retailers money, but also added value to the consumer experience by speeding up checkouts. Over time, as the system proved itself, customers came to appreciate the speed, accuracy, convenience, and cost savings that came with the technology, all of which helped it overcome their initial suspicions.

Selmeier recalled conversations about how the increased profits the UPC could bring the grocery industry would likely be passed along to the consumer. "I'm not implying any collusion," Selmeier said at one meeting with a Kroger executive in 1972, "but this industry has determined on its own that it can operate at 0.68 percent profit after tax and if some technology suddenly comes in to make that 2.68 percent, grocers will use that extra profit to gain market share by reducing prices, having more deals, etc. So it's the consumer that gets the 2 percent improvement to the bottom line" (2009).

In reality, everyone benefited. Retailers indeed passed along savings to their customers, but the industry profit margins began moving upward to the 2 percent range as many predicted.

Tools that drive data insight lead to value. The Universal Product Code provided an efficient way to collect and store data, which enabled improved forecasting and replenishment, improved inventory management, and the development of better intelligence about consumer buying behaviors and patterns.

Innovators don't always stick to a prescribed script. Laurer's fresh perspective on the challenge and his willingness to risk his job on an idea he believed in aren't to be overlooked. IBM, meanwhile, deserves credit for pivoting when it became clear Laurer had come up with something better than other existing options such as RCA's bull's-eye product code. One reason IBM was willing to do this was because it was relatively new to the game.

"IBM did not have an optical bar code or equipment to read optical bar codes on the market at that time," Laurer (2012) noted. "We had no proprietary equipment to sell or protect or make fit the requirements. These facts gave me a chance to start from scratch."

The challenge for future innovators is to adopt this mentality regardless of their current position in the market. Some can start from scratch because that's where they are; others need to be willing to ignore or even destroy their current models to make something better.

Innovations often have an impact beyond their original design. It's also interesting that Laurer and his team never thought they were developing a technology that would have such a global impact. They were focused on solving the problem they were given, but unlocking that door led to hallways and rooms they never imagined existed.

The UPC began as an innovation on the front lines of grocery retail, but in time it spread throughout the retail environment and into many other industries that found unique uses for the technology. In much the same way that laser inventor Theodore Maiman didn't foresee his technology playing a role in scanners and printers, Laurer didn't realize what might become of the UPC.

"We never envisioned the UPC outside of the grocery industry," Laurer said. "We never thought it would become worldwide. We never thought that it would exist after 25 years" (IDHistory 2010a).

An enabling technology that solves a supply chain problem often not only scales as intended, but also rolls out into many other corners of the industry—and other industries, as well.

Links to Other Supply Chain Innovators

Bar code technology was a significant step in the history of supply chain management, adding a twist to the work of other innovators while setting the stage for innovations to come.

For instance, intermodal, the sea container, and the wooden pallet all established new and highly scalable transportation and materials handling standards, while the bar code had a similar impact on data exchange. And Henry Ford's production system centered around the

FIGURE 4.3 A Toyota kanban

Source: Christoph Roser, AllAboutLean.com

organization of work for the workers and the use of technology to enable workers to be more efficient. The bar code provided similar advancements in process efficiencies in the retail environment, while also creating a more customercentric checkout process.

Meanwhile, the lean manufacturing system for which Ohno Taiichi was inducted into the CSCMP Hall of Fame uses kanban cards that often feature bar codes and QR codes. In fact, the QR code was developed by Denso, part of the Toyota group, to contain more information than a bar code. Prior to the inclusion of the QR code, a kanban often featured nine bar codes. Kanban cards (Figure 4.3) are associated with different parts and help trigger replenishment of each part once it is used in production.

"I've often said the most important thing the UPC did was to show the world that bar codes were viable," Laurer said. "After that, there are hundreds of other bar codes in existence today. The automobile VIN code, anyplace you look you'll see other bar codes. . . . The thing the UPC did was show the world that yes, bar codes are here to stay" (Stokel-Walker 2019).

Today's Relevance

Bar codes did more than just help the grocery industry cut costs, operate more efficiently, and lower prices for customers. As journalist Tim Harford noted, it also changed "the balance of power" in the industry.

"By tracking and automating inventory, it made just-in-time deliveries more attractive and lowered the cost of having a wide variety of products," Harford (2017) wrote. "Shops in general—and supermarkets in particular—started to generalize, selling flowers, clothes, and electronic products."

Walmart, which is well known for its technology-driven approach to supply chain management, became an early adopter of bar code technologies. And the success it had using technology to manage its general merchandising stores gave it confidence that it could successfully join the competitive grocery business.

The uses for bar codes also began moving far beyond grocery checkout systems. Among other things, they are used for tracking shipped packages, ISBN codes in books, boarding passes and luggage for trains, planes, and cruise ships, tickets for sporting and entertainment events, store registries, and patients in hospitals. Retailers are finding new uses, as well. Walmart's app, for instance, allows consumers to scan products at home, add it to their shopping lists, and order them for home delivery or pickup at the store.

By 2004, *Fortune* estimated that the bar code was used by 80–90 percent of the top five hundred companies in the United States (Weightman 2015), and in 2019 GS1 estimated that a bar code was scanned more than six billion times daily (Smith 2019).

Along the way, bar codes were developed for cases to make inventory management easier, and the QR code was developed, making information more easily accessible to customers (GS1 2019b). Newer versions of bar codes (including QR codes) have been developed, and radio-frequency identification (RFID), which uses electromagnetic fields to identify and track tags attached to objects, has been widely seen as "a bar code with an antenna."

What's Next

While Laurer's original UPC remains a fixture in retail around the world, bar code technology has continued to evolve to meet the changing needs of consumers and industry. Traditional linear bar codes like Laurer's UPC use varying widths and spacing of parallel lines to represent data. But improvements in printing and scanning have allowed for the emergence of two-dimensional bar codes that can represent much more information.

A two-dimensional (2-D) bar code uses geometric patterns such as dots, hexagons, and rectangles rather than parallel lines. The most common 2-D bar codes are QR codes and DataMatrix codes, and these are more typically used to give consumers access to real-time information about products. For instance, shoppers can scan a QR code to review weekly advertisements at their favorite store, to learn about the product journey of a package of spareribs, or to learn what climate zone is best for the begonias they are considering for their flowerpots. Two-dimensional codes also are being generated for such uses as mobile boarding passes for flights, tickets to a concert, or access to the webpage of a restaurant's menu.

However, as Melanie Nuce, senior vice president for innovation and partnerships of GS1 US, points out, the problem is that multiple codes now often appear on packaging, which can be confusing to consumers and "desensitize" them to the value of the codes. "The time has come to rethink the role of the UPC bar code," Nuce (2021) has written, "and help industry adopt more robust data carriers that support the complex data needs of today's retail environment."

Nuce points out that 82 percent of retailers and 92 percent of brands support transitioning from the UPC to more data-rich 2-D bar codes, according to a study by GS1 US and VDC Research. "The industry's goal is to transition to the new codes by 2027," according to Nuce, "with a temporary period where two codes may exist on product packaging while scanner technology is effectively migrated as well" (2021).

The UPC provides static data, but the 2-D codes open a window into an "information portal" where consumers can engage with products and brands. Not only can consumers learn information about products when they are shopping, but the brands can push out information and promotional offers. At the same time, these bar codes can work with evolving point-of-sale systems that customers use when checking out at stores and that the stores count on for managing inventory.

In 2018, GS1 ratified Digital Link, a Web-enabled bar code that connects physical products with their digital identities by embedding the product's GTIN into a specific web address for the product (Figure 4.4).

Use cases for the 2-D code include nutritional labeling, regulatory disclosures, recall information, product certification information, and

FIGURE 4.4 Example of a GS1 Digital Link URL syntax, including GS1 identifiers

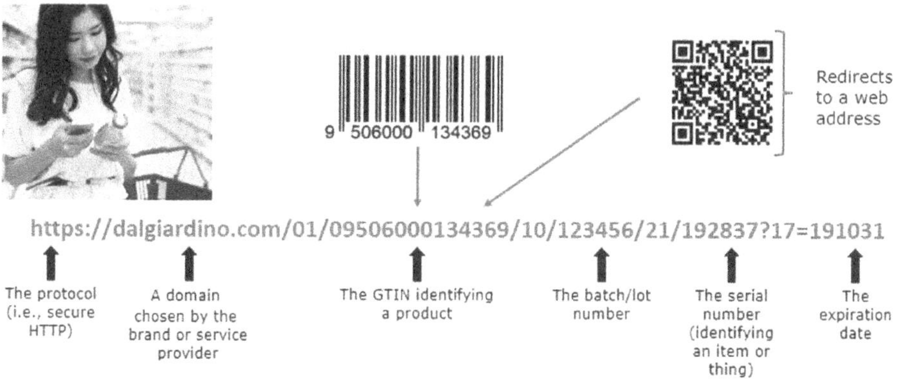
9 506000 134369
Redirects to a web address
https://dalgiardino.com/01/09506000134369/10/123456/21/192837?17=191031
The protocol (i.e., secure HTTP)
A domain chosen by the brand or service provider
The GTIN identifying a product
The batch/lot number
The serial number (identifying an item or thing)
The expiration date

Source: GS1 US CSCMP Annual Conference Presentation 2023, Orlando, Florida

recycling and sustainability information. These use cases enrich the data at the fingertips of consumers and enable manufacturers to keep product information up to date, even after a product has long left the factory. Recalls, for example, can be added to the online product information that the 2-D code takes the consumer to. As a result, industry can move toward "smart packaging."

Moving forward, the bar code is a good reminder of the value of considering the uses of an innovation over the pursuit of technology for technology's sake. While the bar code is widely used today and has multiple uses, the initial purpose was very targeted and industry specific. This made it a worthy investment by the consortium as it developed and scaled the technology.

As with any new technology, considering which specific supply chain objective it can serve and how it can support organizational goals is a critical litmus test. Without it, a technology may just be a shiny new solution in search of a problem.

George Laurer Timeline

1932—Wallace Flint, a Harvard business student, writes a master's thesis proposing a system in which grocery customers would use punch cards to designate items they wanted to purchase and give it to a clerk at the counter who would insert the card into a reader. The reader would activate a conveyor belt system used for bringing the products to the counter, while also recording what was bought.

1948—Bernard Silver, a graduate student at Drexel Institute, overhears the president of a food company asking the business school dean to research a way to capture product information during the checkout process. The dean doesn't pursue the idea, but Silver shares the story with fellow grad student Joe Woodland, and the two begin researching solutions for an automated retail checkout system that could track inventory.

January 1949—Woodland is thinking about Morse code while moving his fingers through the sand on a beach in Miami when he has an epiphany about using a bar/space pattern for a scannable bar code system.

October 20, 1949—Woodland and Silver file a patent application for a "classifying apparatus and method." They used a circular bull's-eye pattern because they believed it would be easier to read by a scanner from any direction.

1951—Woodland takes a job with IBM.

October 7, 1952—A patent is granted to Woodland and Silver and they build the first working bar code reader, a massive contraption that requires a 500-watt incandescent lightbulb and an RCA 935 photomultiplier tube connected to an oscilloscope. It worked, but it was not economically feasible to use given the technologies of the day.

1950s—Computer engineer David Collins puts "thin and thick lines" on railway cars that can be read by a trackside scanner. Collins tries to get Sylvania Corp to back the idea of using automated coding beyond railroads. Sylvania says no, and he quits to found Computer Identics Corporation.

July 16, 1960—Theodore Maiman, a research scientist with Hughes Aircraft Company, demonstrates the first working device for Light Amplification by Stimulated Emission of Radiation, aka a laser. "They imagined it would have many applications in science and communications, in industry for cutting and welding, and in medicine for delicate surgery. But, as Maiman wrote, 'I did not foresee the supermarket check-out scanner or the printer.'"

1962—Woodland and Silver turn down a lower offer from IBM and sell their patent to Philco for $15,000; Philco later sells it to RCA.

1963—Silver dies at the age of 38.

1966—A Kroger booklet ends with a challenge: "Just dreaming a little . . . could an optical scanner read the price and total the sale. . . . Faster service, more productive service is needed desperately. We solicit your help."

1969—The patent expires on the original Woodland/Silver concept.

1969—Computer Identics, founded by David Collins, installs two bar code reading systems, one at a General Motors plant in Michigan and the other at a distribution facility owned by General Trading Company in Carlsbad, New Jersey.

September 1969—Members of the administrative systems committee of the Grocery Manufacturers of America (GMA) meet with their counterparts from the National Association of Food Chains (NAFC) to discuss a joint effort to create a standard workable bar code.

1970—An industry consortium establishes an ad hoc committee that sets guidelines for bar code development and a "symbol selection" subcommittee that is charged with creating a standardized approach.

Spring 1971—RCA demonstrates a bull's-eye–shaped bar code during a grocery industry meeting, drawing the attention of the crowd, including IBM executives who would later transfer Woodland to an IBM facility in North Carolina to help with the company's own bar code project.

March 9, 1971—The original ad hoc committee forms two subcommittees: the Symbol Standardization Committee chaired by Alan Haberman and the Code Management Subcommittee.

March 31, 1971—The ad hoc committee decides on the Universal Product Code, a ten-digit code with a check digit. The Symbol Selection Committee calls for the final recommendation for a symbol to be made by April 1, 1973. The parameters for the symbol are 1) no larger than 1.5 inches square, 2) able to be printed with the common label printing technology, 3) readable from any direction, and 4) fewer than 1 in 20,000 undetected errors.

December 1971—The Uniform Grocery Product Code Council (UGPCC) is incorporated. It has three initial tasks: select a company to manage the codes or the distribution of the numbers, develop a corporate structure for the UGPCC to supervise the company selected for distribution, and figure out how to fund the project going forward.

July 3, 1972—The first automated checkout stands, installed at Kroger Kenwood Plaza in Cincinnati, scan RCA's bull's-eye–style bar code based on the Woodland/Silver model.

1973—Laurer tells his boss he has abandoned the circular model for a rectangular approach. "I didn't do what you asked," he says.

March 30, 1973—Scientists from MIT evaluate the proposed symbologies for the UPC on behalf of the Symbol Selection Committee, and Laurer's rectangular code prevails.

April 3, 1973—IBM's bar code is officially adopted as the standard Universal Product Code, transforming bar codes "from a technological curiosity into a business juggernaut."

October 11, 1973—IBM begins marketing the IBM 3660, which includes a point-of-sale digital cash register with a checkout scanner that can read the UPC symbol.

September 1974—The UPGCC becomes the Uniform Product Code Council (UPCC) and is given authority to administer the bar code. The UPCC is now known as GS1.

June 26, 1974—A ten-pack of Wrigley's Juicy Fruit gum becomes the first item marked with a UPC code to be scanned during a demonstration at Troy's Marsh Supermarket in Troy, Ohio, using checkout equipment provided by National Cash Register. The gum is priced at 69 cents, but Marsh's price is 67 cents, which is the price the scanner reads.

1976—A thirteenth digit is added to the code, enabling use of the identification system outside the United States.

1978—Fewer than 1 percent of grocery stores in the United States have scanners. That figure rose to 10 percent in 1981, 33 percent by 1984, and more than 60 percent by 1993.

1983—ITF-14 bar codes are used on cases to make inventory easier to manage.

1994—The QR code is developed in Japan, adding a new dimension to bar code use by allowing information to be more easily shared directly with customers.

1998—GS1 introduces the DataBar, a code small enough to use on items such as fruit and jewelry.

2004—*Fortune* estimates that the bar code is used by 80–90 percent of the top five hundred companies in the United States.

June 24, 2019—GS1, the standards organization that administers the UPC bar codes, estimates that a bar code is scanned more than six billion times daily.

References

Business Week. 1973. "A Standard Labeling Code for Food." April 7, 71.

CSCMP. 2017. "George Laurer Interview—CSCMP 2017 Supply Chain Hall of Fame Inductee." October 2. YouTube video, 4:32. https://youtu.be/CDdrrvEvYsk?si=rGe8P4VDkQPeHthw.

GS1. n.d. "A Brief History/Timeline of GS1 US and the U.P.C." Internal memorandum. Used with permission.

GS1. 2019a. "George Laurer, Who Co-invented the Bar Code, Died at Age 94." December 16. https://www.gs1.org/resources/articles/george-laurer-who-co-invented-barcode-died-age-94 .

GS1. 2019b. "Happy Birthday, Bar Code! Learn about the Bar Code's Impact over 45 Years." Accessed August 4, 2020. https://www.gs1us.org/DesktopModules/Bring2mind/DMX/Download.aspx?Command=Core_Download&EntryId=1699&language=en-US&PortalId=0&TabId=134 (site no longer available).

Harford, T. 2017. "How the Bar Code Changed Retailing and Manufacturing." BBC World Service, January 23.

IBM. n.d. "UPC: The Transformation of Retail, IBM 100: Icons of Progress." Accessed February 9, 2021. https://www.ibm.com/ibm/history/ibm100/us/en/icons/upc/.

IDHistory. 2010a. "George Laurer on UPC Lessons Learned." September 3. YouTube video, 2:17. https://youtu.be/YnB9b-7xYNE.

IDHistory. 2010b. "George Laurer Discusses Some of the Challenges in Creating the New U.P.C. Bar Code." September 5. YouTube video, 3:58. https://youtu.be/g6CvNMZZhHQ.

Kennedy, P. 2013. "Who Made That Universal Product Code?" *New York Times Magazine*, January 4. https://www.nytimes.com/2013/01/06/magazine/who-made-that-universal-product-code.html.

Laurer, George. 2012. *Engineering Was Fun.* 3rd ed. Raleigh, NC: Lulu Press.

Metz, Cade. 2012. "Why the Bar Code Will Always Be the Mark of the Beast." Wired.com, December 28. https://www.wired.com/2012/12/upc-mark-of-the-beast/.

Nuce, Melanie. 2021. "Why the Barcode Has to Evolve," CSCMP Hot Topics. April 14. https://cscmp.org/store/detail.aspx?id=HT21-GS1-APR.

Roser, Christoph. 2017. "Anatomy of the Toyota Kanban." https://www.allaboutlean.com/toyota-kanban/.

Seideman, T. 1993. "Bar Codes Sweep the World." *American Heritage's Invention & Technology Magazine* 8, no. 4 (Spring), 1–5. https://www.academia.edu/2484615/Bar codes_sweep_the_world.

Selmeier, B. 2009. *Spreading the Barcode.* (n.p.): William Selmeier.

Smith, H. 2019. "George Laurer, an Inventor of the Modern Bar Code, Dies at 94." *Washington Post*, December 10.

Stokel-Walker, Chris. 2019. "Beep Beep: The History of George Laurer and the Bar Code." OneZero.com, December 10. https://onezero.medium.com/beep-beep-the-history-of-george-laurer-and-the-barcode-3522a15405ea.

Weightman, G. 2015. "The History of the Bar Code." *Smithsonian*, September.

Woodland, Norman J., and Bernard Silver. 1952. Classifying apparatus and method. US Patent 2612994A.

CHAPTER 5

Elizabeth Dole

Birth: July 29, 1936
Titles: Secretary of Transportation under Ronald Reagan (1983–1987);
Secretary of Labor under George H. W. Bush (1989–1990); US senator
(2003–2009) representing North Carolina; president of the American Red
Cross (1991–1999)
Hall of Fame Induction: 2019
Key Supply Chain Innovation: Advocated for expanding the roles and
influence of women, people with disabilities, and minorities in the trans-
portation industry; led efforts to improve safety on American highways.

Elizabeth Dole shattered a number of glass ceilings as she blazed a trail from the small town of Salisbury in western North Carolina to the halls of elite academic institutions such as Duke, Oxford, and Harvard and throughout a career of public service that took her to the highest levels of politics.

She was the first female US secretary of transportation (in Ronald Reagan's administration), the first woman to lead a branch of the US military (the Coast Guard), the first woman to lead two different cabinet-level departments (Transportation and Labor) under two different US presidents (Reagan and George H. W. Bush), and the first female US senator for North Carolina. She also was the second woman to serve as president of the American Red Cross and the first since its founder, Clara Barton, retired in 1904.

The impact Dole had on transportation, however, had less to do with her breaking new ground as the first woman to hold roles traditionally held by men and more to do with the overall influence she had on politics, industry, and society. This makes her unique among members of the Supply Chain Hall of Fame. While most owe their inclusion to specific innovations—Henry Ford's assembly line, for instance, or George Laurer's development of bar code technology—Dole was a conduit for change in several important areas.

Long before environmental, social, and corporate governance (ESG) became part of the corporate lexicon, Dole was advocating for, modeling, and implementing higher ESG standards in the organizations she led. She was intentional about creating opportunities for women to advance into leadership roles in the transportation industry, she helped reshape policy to emphasize and improve safety on national highways, she championed environmental legislation, and she effectively displayed an inclusive style of leadership that was uncommon for its time (see handwritten talking points summarizing the secretary's agenda in Figures 5.1 and 5.2).

Dole's industry innovation took a form that's hard to define by pointing to a singular technology, process, or event. But instituting meaningful policies and programs, changing hearts, minds, and attitudes, and leading by word and example are also ways to impact an industry for the better. That's the Hall of Fame legacy of Elizabeth Dole.

FIGURE 5.1 Handwritten speaking notes by Secretary Elizabeth Hanford Dole for speech on September 29, 1983, Williamsburg, Virginia, Seminar for Prospective Women Managers

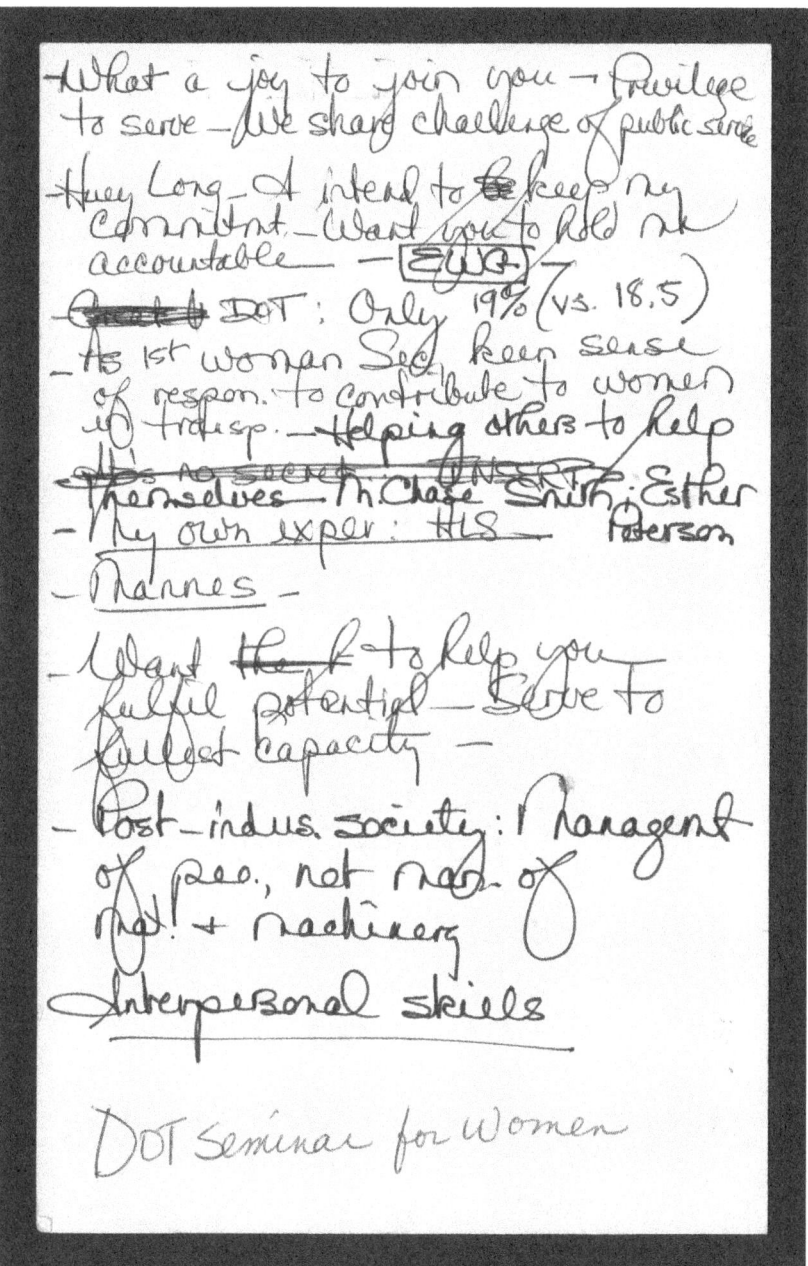

Source: The Elizabeth Dole Collection, Robert J. Dole Institute of Politics, University of Kansas

FIGURE 5.2 Handwritten speaking notes by Secretary Elizabeth Hanford Dole for speech on September 29, 1983, Williamsburg, Virginia, Seminar for Prospective Women Managers

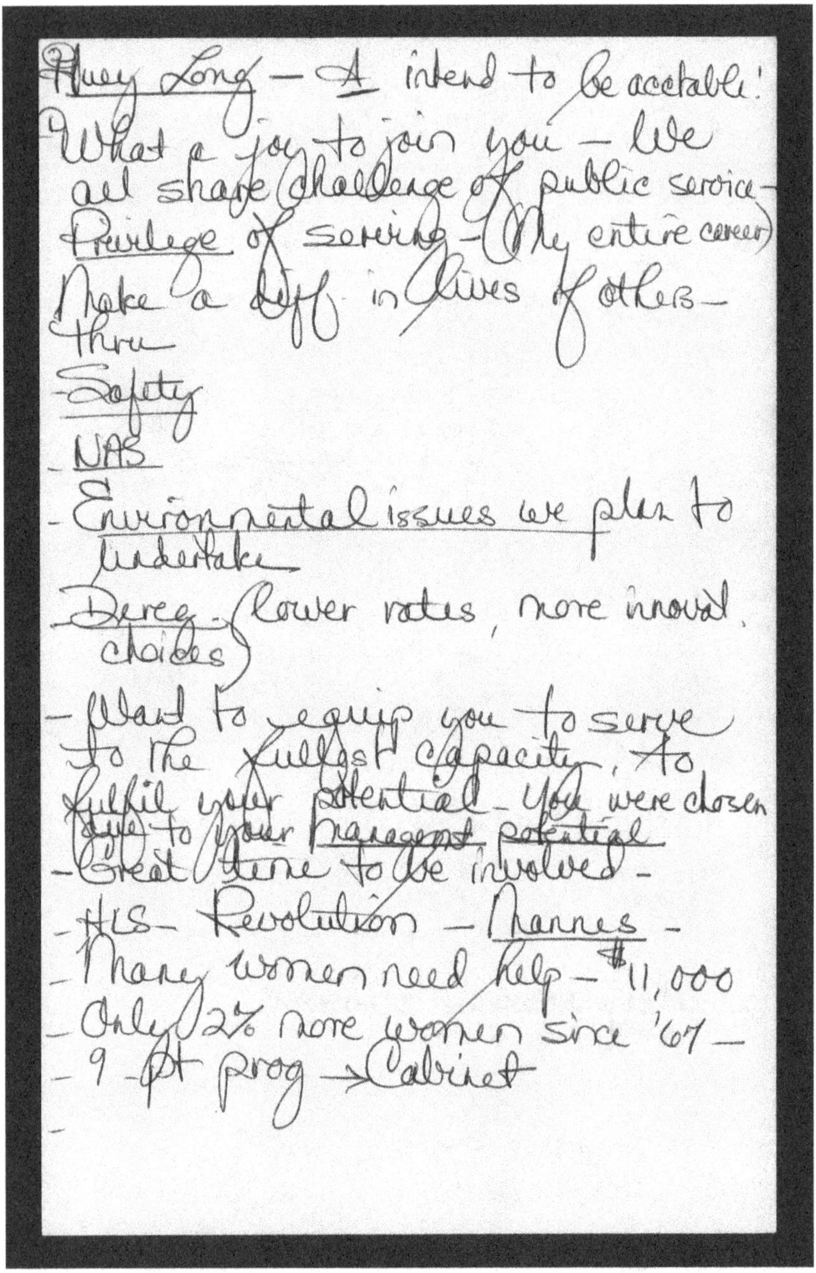

Huey Long — I intend to be acctable!
What a joy to join you — We
all share challenge of public service —
Privilege of serving — (My entire career)
Make a diff in lives of others —
thru —
Safety
- NAS
- Environmental issues we plan to undertake
Dereg. (lower rates, more innovat. choices)
- Want to equip you to serve to the fullest capacity, to fulfill your potential — You were chosen due to your managemt potential
- Great time to be involved —
- HLS — Revolution — Mannes —
- Many women need help — $11,000
- Only 2% more women since '67 —
- 9 pt prog → Cabinet
-

Source: The Elizabeth Dole Collection, Robert J. Dole Institute of Politics, University of Kansas

The Ten-Point Plan

A few years after Dole left the Department of Transportation (DOT), she was walking through an airport terminal when someone she'd never met asked for a minute of her time. This wasn't unusual for such a well-known public figure, but this particular interruption brought with it a heart-warming message that Dole never forgot. "Mrs. Dole, I just wanted you to know I'm the manager of this airport now," the woman said, "and it's because I was in the women's program at DOT" (Rainey 2007). Similar encounters happened with at least two other airport managers in the years following Dole's tenure as secretary of transportation, and she also heard from women who were in a variety of other leadership roles in the industry and within the DOT.

Such expressions of gratitude, in fact, began almost as soon as she took office. After a speech at a breakfast for women DOT employees, for instance, she received a handwritten note from one of the attendees thanking her "for the inspiration you've given me and thousands upon thousands of other women across the United States" (Plymate, n.d.). That's because the women's program she created had a broad impact on gender equality in the transportation sectors of the supply chain management profession.

Dole improved upon some existing programs at the DOT and added new ones to create what became known as her ten-point program for increasing opportunities for women in the transportation industry. "As the first woman Secretary of Transportation," Dole said during a 1983 speech to a DOT seminar for prospective women managers, "I feel a keen sense of responsibility to make sure I can make a contribution to women in transportation" (E. Dole 1983c).

It was a calling she repeated often during her time as secretary. Within her first few months on the job, she began regularly citing data that backed up the reasons for why such a contribution was necessary. She pointed out that in 1980 women comprised about 16 percent of the overall workforce in transportation—33 percent in aviation, 28 percent in transit, 13 percent in trucking and maritime jobs, and just 8 percent in railroad jobs (see Figure 5.3).

"Clearly, there is substantial room for improvement," she said during a May 16, 1983, speech to the Women's Transportation Seminar. "And the place to begin is at the Department of Transportation itself" (1983a).

FIGURE 5.3 Remarks prepared for delivery by Secretary Elizabeth Hanford Dole to the Women's Transportation Seminar, Washington, DC, May 16, 1983

- MUCH HAS CHANGED SINCE ~~THEN~~. *I finished HS in '65:* DOUBLE-DIGIT INFLATION OF THE 1970'S FORCED MANY WOMEN INTO THE LABOR MARKET FOR THE FIRST TIME. DIVORCED WOMEN JOINED THE ECONOMY AT THE SAME TIME, UNTIL WE REACHED POINT WHERE 63 PERCENT OF WOMEN WITH CHILDREN BETWEEN THE AGES OF 6 AND 17 WERE IN AMERICA'S LABOR FORCE IN 1982.
- " *(MARRYA) MANNES* NOBODY OBJECTS TO A WOMAN BEING A GOOD WRITER OR SCULPTOR OR GENETICIST IF, AT THE SAME TIME, SHE MANAGES TO BE A GOOD WIFE, A GOOD MOTHER, GOOD-LOOKING, GOOD TEMPERED, WELL-DRESSED, WELL-GROOMED AND UNAGGRESSIVE."
- THE MEMBERS OF THIS ORGANIZATION OFFER LIVING PROOF THAT WOMEN HAVE THE SKILLS NEEDED IN TRANSPORTATION. BUT WE ALSO HAVE OUR WORK CUT OUT FOR US IN GETTING THAT IDEA ACCEPTED.
- FOR INSTANCE, WOMEN TODAY MAKE UP 33 PERCENT OF THE AVIATION WORKFORCE; 28 PERCENT IN TRANSIT. UNFORTUNATELY, THEY ARE THE HIGH POINTS. FOR THE TRUCKING AND MARITIME TRADES, THE FIGURES DROP TO 13 PERCENT. AND IN RRs, WOMEN COMPRISE ONLY 8 PERCENT OF THE WORKFORCE.
- SUBSTANTIAL ROOM FOR IMPROVEMENT. PLACE TO BEGIN IS AT THE D.O.T. ITSELF.
- WHEN THE DEPARTMENT WAS ESTABLISHED IN 1967, 18.5 PERCENT OF TOTAL WORKFORCE WAS FEMALE. TODAY, 16 YEARS LATER, WOMEN STILL REPRESENT LESS THAN 20 PERCENT OF OUR PERSONNEL STRENGTH. SOME GAINS AT MGMT. LEVELS HAVE OCCURRED. BUT WOMEN IN GRADES GS-13 AND ABOVE STILL MAKE UP ONLY ONE PERCENT OF THE TOTAL. NOW DEVELOPING SPECIFIC RECOMMENDATIONS TO IMPROVE THE STATUS OF WOMEN IN THE DEPARTMENT. THESE ARE JUST SOME OF THE OPTIONS WE ARE LOOKING AT:

  --INCREASING THE OPPORTUNITIES FOR WOMEN TO ENTER PROFESSIONAL AND TECHNICAL OCCUPATIONS AT THE ENTRY LEVEL;

  --PREPARING WOMEN IN MID-LEVEL GRADES FOR MORE RESPONSIBLE MGMT. POSITIONS; AND

Source: The Elizabeth Dole Collection, Robert J. Dole Institute of Politics, University of Kansas

When the Department of Transportation was established in 1967, 18.5 percent of its employees were women. When Dole took office in 1983, the number had risen to only 19 percent. To improve those numbers, Dole knew women needed more training to gain the skills and experiences required for better jobs, as well as more opportunities to put those skills and experiences to good use. Thus, she formalized a plan that began with three priorities—increasing the opportunities for women to enter professional and technical occupations at the entry level, preparing women in midlevel grades for more responsible management positions, and providing opportunities for women who were already in management positions to improve their skills and move into the senior executive service (E. Dole 1983a).

"I asked in the first weeks of my tenure at the Department for a program addressing the needs of women employees from entry level jobs through senior management positions—a program which cuts across the Department's organizational lines," she said in her May 16 speech (1983a). "In early May I attended a Cabinet Council meeting chaired by the President to discuss ways to improve the status of women in Federal government management positions. Needless to say, I was delighted to report that we were already developing a program at DOT. I have been asked to brief the Council, which I will do in the near future. I look forward to the briefing because I am very enthusiastic about our program and anxious to present a model which other departments can follow."

Within a few months the three initiatives had grown to ten, nine of which were shared in a brochure titled "The Secretary of Transportation's Initiatives to Improve Opportunities for Women." The brochure highlighted programs in three categories: entry-level opportunities, management training opportunities, and opportunities to enhance qualifications for senior management positions.

The entry-level opportunities consisted of the Upward Mobility Program, the Graduated Cooperative Education Program, and the Air Traffic Controller Training Program. The management category offered the Secretary of Transportation's Seminar for Prospective Women Managers, the Mobility Assignment Training Program, and the Non-DOT Management Development Program. And the programs for enhancing senior management qualifications were the Intergovernmental Mobility Assignments, the Senior Executive Service Candidate Development Program, and the Management Skills Seminar (see Figure 5.4).

FIGURE 5.4 The table of contents from "The Secretary of Transportation's Initiatives to Improve Opportunities for Women," a brochure published in 1983

Contents

"The success of this effort depends largely upon your own participation, for it is your career we seek to advance, your aspirations we want to realize," she told employees in a letter in the brochure (see Figure 5.5). "Working in partnership, we can bring life to Helen Keller's maxim: 'One can never consent to creep when one feels an impulse to soar.' Together we can soar" (DOT, n.d., "Secretary of Transportation's Initiative").

She soon began referring to it as the ten-point plan, with the tenth program most likely involving career planning for employees with limited advancement opportunities.

She was quick to operationalize each aspect of the program. In fiscal year 1984, for instance, the department held ten sessions of its Seminar for Prospective Women Managers (see Figure 5.6). And another program created rotational assignments to broaden the range of experiences for women. Someone working in the Federal Railroad Administration, for example, would go work for the Federal Highway Administration.

Dole presented details on the ten-point program during at least one Reagan cabinet meeting (September 8, 1983), where she received the president's backing. She also "suggested that it be adopted at other federal agencies" (E. Dole 1983c). And she spoke about it during speeches all over the country.

Progress followed. In a speech in October 1984, she noted that 20.5 percent of the DOT workforce was women. That 1.5-percentage-point increase came in less than two years, three times more than it had increased in the previous sixteen years (E. Dole 1984b).

Progress also was seen in the specifics of various programs. Seventy-five women in clerical positions, for instance, had attended a career planning course during those first two years. Thirty-six of the fifty designated upward mobility slots had been filled by women. Of the 247 students in a co-op program that prepared candidates for the air traffic controller program, 41 percent were women. More than three hundred women had taken the Seminar for Prospective Women Managers. And the Senior Executive Service Candidate Development Program included ten women, up from just two in the previous class.

By April 1985, women constituted 21 percent of the department's full-time workforce, and by August 1985 this figure was up to 23 percent—an improvement of four percentage points in less than three years

FIGURE 5.5 A letter to employees by Elizabeth Dole in "The Secretary of Transportation's Initiatives to Improve Opportunities for Women," a brochure published in 1983

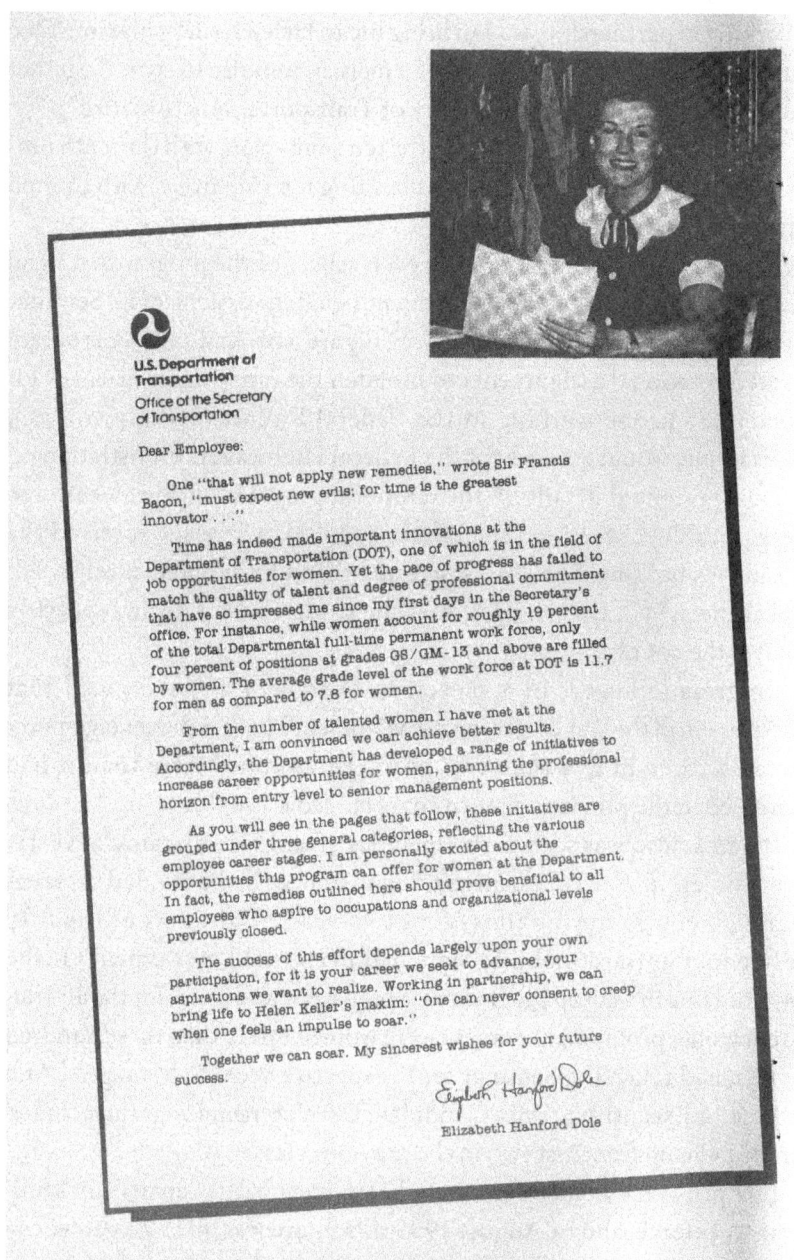

U.S. Department of Transportation
Office of the Secretary
of Transportation

Dear Employee:

One "that will not apply new remedies," wrote Sir Francis Bacon, "must expect new evils; for time is the greatest innovator . . ."

Time has indeed made important innovations at the Department of Transportation (DOT), one of which is in the field of job opportunities for women. Yet the pace of progress has failed to match the quality of talent and degree of professional commitment that have so impressed me since my first days in the Secretary's office. For instance, while women account for roughly 19 percent of the total Departmental full-time permanent work force, only four percent of positions at grades GS/GM-15 and above are filled by women. The average grade level of the work force at DOT is 11.7 for men as compared to 7.8 for women.

From the number of talented women I have met at the Department, I am convinced we can achieve better results. Accordingly, the Department has developed a range of initiatives to increase career opportunities for women, spanning the professional horizon from entry level to senior management positions.

As you will see in the pages that follow, these initiatives are grouped under three general categories, reflecting the various employee career stages. I am personally excited about the opportunities this program can offer for women at the Department. In fact, the remedies outlined here should prove beneficial to all employees who aspire to occupations and organizational levels previously closed.

The success of this effort depends largely upon your own participation, for it is your career we seek to advance, your aspirations we want to realize. Working in partnership, we can bring life to Helen Keller's maxim: "One can never consent to creep when one feels an impulse to soar."

Together we can soar. My sincerest wishes for your future success.

Elizabeth Hanford Dole

Elizabeth Hanford Dole

FIGURE 5.6 The 1983–1984 scheduled sessions for the Seminar for Prospective Women Managers

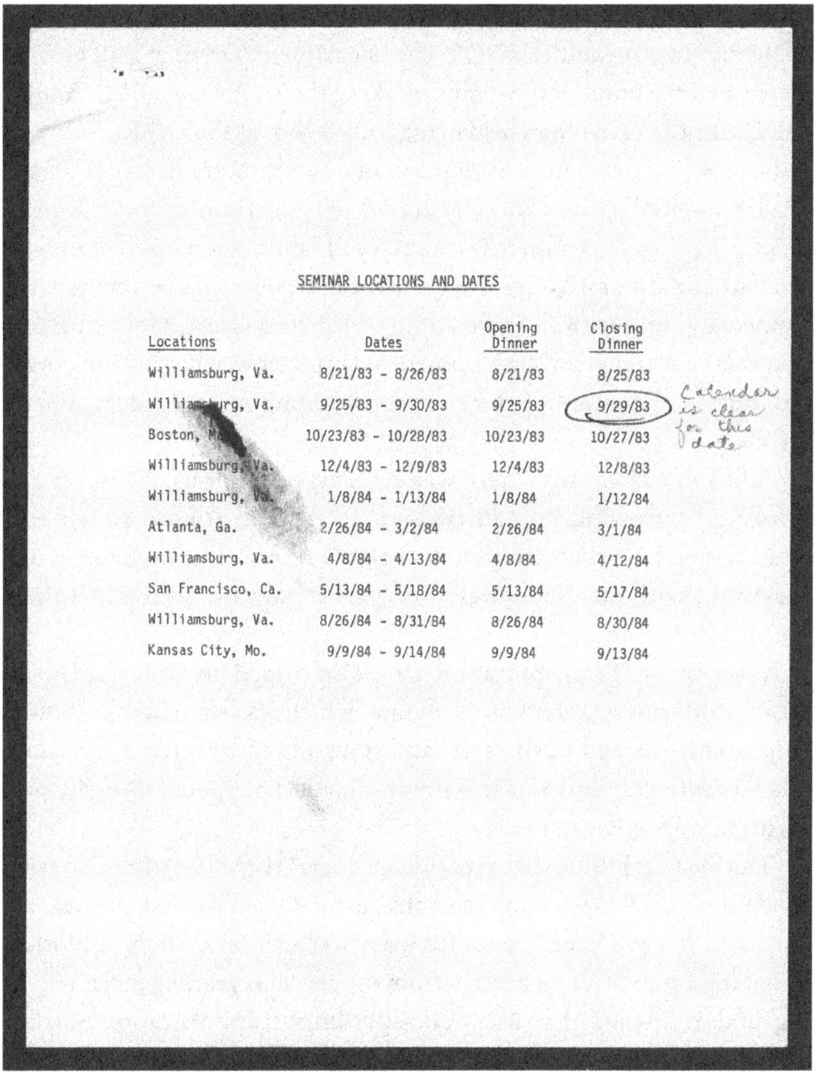

SEMINAR LOCATIONS AND DATES

Locations	Dates	Opening Dinner	Closing Dinner
Williamsburg, Va.	8/21/83 - 8/26/83	8/21/83	8/25/83
Williamsburg, Va.	9/25/83 - 9/30/83	9/25/83	9/29/83
Boston, Ma.	10/23/83 - 10/28/83	10/23/83	10/27/83
Williamsburg, Va.	12/4/83 - 12/9/83	12/4/83	12/8/83
Williamsburg, Va.	1/8/84 - 1/13/84	1/8/84	1/12/84
Atlanta, Ga.	2/26/84 - 3/2/84	2/26/84	3/1/84
Williamsburg, Va.	4/8/84 - 4/13/84	4/8/84	4/12/84
San Francisco, Ca.	5/13/84 - 5/18/84	5/13/84	5/17/84
Williamsburg, Va.	8/26/84 - 8/31/84	8/26/84	8/30/84
Kansas City, Mo.	9/9/84 - 9/14/84	9/9/84	9/13/84

Calendar is clear for this date [handwritten note pointing to 9/29/83]

Source: The Elizabeth Dole Collection, Robert J. Dole Institute of Politics, University of Kansas

(E. Dole 1985a). "We were able to get it up 4 percentage points," she said, "which doesn't sound like a lot, but when you've got 100,000 in the workforce it was a lot of women" (Rainey 2007).

These women weren't just getting more opportunities; they were making the most of them. At the DOT annual award ceremony in

1985, more than sixty of the awards went to women, including seven silver medals for meritorious achievement and fifty-four for excellence (DOT 1985).

By the time she left the DOT, the department had seen a 10 percent increase in the number of women working there (B. Dole 2010). And by 1987 nearly 1,700 women held management jobs at the DOT.

Dole would develop similar programs as Secretary of Labor and as head of the Red Cross. Not only did she develop training and advancement programs for women as secretary of labor, but 62 percent of her recommendations to President Bush for senior appointments were women and minorities. And as head of the Red Cross, Dole created a program that allowed young women and minorities who showed potential to serve as apprentices for the organization's senior leaders, including Dole.

"They could go anywhere we went, travel with us, sit in on any meeting," Dole said. "I had two young African American women, and I remember when we went to Atlanta to see Coretta Scott King, they went with me. They were just part of anything I did" (Rainey 2007).

As secretary of transportation, Dole also helped promote the DOT's Women's Business Enterprise Program, which was launched in 1980 to help women-owned businesses land state and federal transportation-related contracts. This was an early version of the supplier diversity programs that are common today.

"During fiscal 1983, states receiving Federal Highway Administration funds awarded $255 million in contracts to women-owned businesses," Dole said at a 1984 conference for women's business owners in Florida. "That was up about eight percent from the previous year. Agencies receiving funds from the Urban Mass Transportation Administration awarded $48 million in contracts to women-owned firms. The Department, in its direct procurements, distributed $26 million to women-owned companies in fiscal 1983, almost double the amount awarded the year before. And we'll keep going!" (1984a).

And, indeed, the federal government has continued to keep this going, making spending with diverse suppliers a common requirement in its requests for proposals.

Shake Ups in Safety

In early October 1983, Dole made a late adjustment to the conclusion of her speech to the American Association of State Highway and Transportation Officials in Denver.

First, she quoted historian Arnold Toynbee, who said, "Civilization is a movement and not a condition: A voyage, not a harbor." Then she added, "Transportation, I suggest, is both a movement and a voyage. We are propelled by change, and innovation is the only safe harbor we will ever know. I look forward to sharing the ride with you, and to smoothing the journey that leads to an even better, safer system of transportation—the finest in our history. I want your help—and I promise you my own" (E. Dole 1983d).

It was an eloquent expression of what many came to see as her signature agenda as secretary of transportation. While her work as an advocate for gender equality was her passion and had a substantial impact, it didn't receive much attention from the media at the time and typically has been undervalued by historians. On the other hand, her "trifecta" of public safety initiatives—seat belt laws, the federal standard of age twenty-one for legal drinking, and air bags—were and are much more well known because those initiatives were more widely reported and had a more direct impact on the lives of all citizens.

"Because of your personal emphasis on transportation safety, it is now a national priority," President Reagan (1987) wrote to Dole when she stepped down as secretary in 1987 so that she could work full time on her husband's presidential campaign. "Countless lives have been saved and crippling injuries prevented on our highways, railroads and in the air because of your leadership. Drunk driving is declining and seat belt use is increasing, drugs and alcohol have been declared off limits to transportation, and vigilance over our air system has never been greater. We have increased competition in industries that for years were stifled by government regulation during a time when travel has never been safer."

Highlights of Dole's efforts to make America's transportation systems safer include many safety aspects that we now all assume as a standard. But Dole helped set those lasting standards (B. Dole 2010; National Safety Council, n.d.):

Rail

- She issued a rule ordering drug and alcohol testing of rail employees after accidents.
- She ordered upgrades that strengthened three thousand rail tank cars carrying liquid flammables.

Air

- She implemented aircraft safety rules in 1983 that ensured seats were less flammable, improved aircraft cabin evacuation with low-level lights, and reduced the danger of fire in lavatories.
- She initiated a program of fourteen thousand safety inspections of airlines, including an additional in-depth inspection of forty-three airlines. The number of Federal Aviation Administration (FAA) safety inspectors increased by 60 percent from 1984 to 1987. The agency also updated its inspector handbook for the first time in twenty-eight years.
- Her tougher aviation security measures, which included adding more air marshals and enhancing surveillance of luggage and cargo, were adopted by European transport ministers.
- She strengthened aviation safety by requiring collision avoidance warning systems in commercial aircraft and requiring general aviation aircraft to use advanced transponders in heavy traffic areas.

Highways

- In 1983 she mandated high-mounted brake lights on cars. The "Dole lights," as they were called, cost less than twenty dollars per vehicle and eliminated an estimated nine hundred thousand crashes annually.
- She led a widespread effort to eliminate drunk driving, particularly among the nation's youth. She was a strong support of legislation that standardized twenty-one as the legal drinking age, eliminating different age requirements in different states.
- In 1984 she issued a safety rule that resolved a twenty-year controversy over automatic crash protection in cars. It called for a phased-in requirement for air bags unless states covering at least two-thirds of the US population enacted seat belt laws. She also provided incentives for auto manufacturers to develop, test, and offer air bags in automobiles. This led to the adoption of mandatory safety belt use laws in

forty-nine states and installation of air bags in more than two hundred million vehicles. Here efforts on this initiative included parking a car with an air bag in the Rose Garden of the White House so that the cabinet could get familiar with the technology.

• She campaigned for and helped implement the Commercial Motor Vehicle Safety Act of 1986.

It's worth noting that the Commercial Motor Vehicle Safety Act of 1986 had a significant impact on training and accountability in the trucking sector of the transportation industry. At the time, twenty states only required a regular driver's license to operate a big-rig truck, which meant drivers had different levels of training. And because truck drivers often carried licenses from multiple states, a suspended license due to violations in one state didn't prevent them from driving. They simply used a license from another state.

The 1986 legislation, however, empowered the DOT to establish "minimum federal standards for the licensing, testing, qualifications and classifications of commercial motor vehicle operators, and additional regulations for such operators who transport hazardous materials" (US Congress 1986). Among other things, it led to regulations prohibiting truck drivers from possessing more than one operator's license. All of this helped ensure that better-trained drivers were on the roads and that drivers who had proven themselves dangerous couldn't continue to drive (see Figure 5.7).

Dole also faced the challenge of virtually rebuilding the air traffic controller workforce. In 1981, just a few years before Dole became secretary of transportation, the Professional Air Traffic Controllers Association (PATCO) called a strike to protest what its thirteen thousand members considered to be unfair wages and long hours. Roughly seven thousand flights were canceled that day, and President Reagan told the union members to return to work within forty-eight hours or they would lose their jobs. Two days later he followed through on that threat and fired more than eleven thousand of the air traffic controllers who had gone on strike.

Airplanes began flying again, but the department was in desperate need of new air traffic controllers. By 1985, when Dole was secretary, the department was up to 74 percent of the number of controllers it needed, which was just shy of where it had been (80 percent) prior to the strike (Domestic Policy Council 1985).

FIGURE 5.7 A background briefing for a 1987 Budget Overview Hearing

FMVSS 208 - OCCUPANT RESTRAINT PROGRAM PROGRESS

DRAFT

QUESTION: When you announced your decision regarding FMVSS 208 automatic restraints, you indicated that a program would begin immediately to encourage use of occupant restraints and to provide technical assistance to States considering mandatory use laws. What progress has been made in implementing the program?

ANSWER: MAJOR POINTS:

1. Sixteen States[1] and the District of Columbia have now enacted mandatory safety belt use laws, including 14 and D.C. in the last year. That number is expected to increase significantly in 1986.

2. Safety belt use (as measured in the 19-cities survey) increased in the first half of 1985 over the first half of 1984 by over 6 percentage points (from below 13% to 19.4%).

3. Ten States with belt use laws received program implementation grants from DOT in 1985 to assist with education and evaluation. The States are Connecticut, New York, New Jersey,[2] North Carolina, Michigan, Illinois, Missouri, Nebraska, Texas, and New Mexico. More are expected in 1986.

4. In the last year, 30 State workshops to assist community safety belt and child safety seat program managers have been sponsored by DOT. A national meeting to train managers was held in November 1985.

5. A technical assistance program to help the States with implementing and evaluating State programs (principally to conduct safety belt use surveys) has been developed.

6. National organizations (principally health, education, and medical) are sponsoring, with DOT support, nearly 400 State and local projects to stimulate community-based programs. A national training workshop was held in July.

---

[1] As of January 13, a usage bill has passed the Ohio legislature and awaits the Governor's approval. If signed, the total number of States will rise to 17.

[2] An article in the Philadelphia Inquirer dated 1/14/86 indicates that fatalities have increased in New Jersey since the mandatory safety belt use law became effective in March 1985 (article attached).

Source: The Elizabeth Dole Collection, Robert J. Dole Institute of Politics, University of Kansas

"The rapid expansion of the airline industry, the stimulus of deregulation, and the air traffic controller strike have provided a period of unprecedented challenge to the air traffic control system," Dole said. "The air traffic control workforce has been rebuilt to the level established immediately following the 1981 PATCO strike. The system is now handling more traffic than before the strike and is doing so without system constraints and without abnormal delays. In this process of rebuilding the controller workforce, safety has not been compromised. Indeed, over the greater part of this period accident rates have been down, and the differing causes of the recent crashes do not point to a problem with the air traffic control system" (1985b).

Environmental Contributions

Some of the safety issues Dole championed, such as the DOT order to strengthen rail tank cars that carried liquid flammables, had a positive impact on the environment. But she also developed and pushed an agenda specific to environmental issues.

This effort went through a different cycle than her women's initiative. While the women's initiative grew from three to nine to ten elements, the environmental program went from more than two dozen down to just three.

In her first year as secretary of transportation, Dole established a departmental steering committee to develop environmental initiatives in five areas: highway/transit, aviation noise, historic preservation, hazardous materials, and oil pollution. By February 1984, her staff had come up with around twenty proposed initiatives for the committee to consider (see Figure 5.8). "Considering the sense of urgency that that Secretary has conveyed to me," Jeffrey Shane (1984), deputy assistant secretary for policy and international affairs, wrote to the committee, "I request that you provide me with concurrence and any comments by COB Wednesday, March 7."

Under "highway/transit" initiatives, there were proposals for a policy statement, ride-sharing, truck noise, transit noise, publicity, and highway beautification. The three aviation initiatives all addressed noise issues (aircraft, airports, and helicopters). Six programs, plus an "other" category, were listed under hazardous materials and seven under oil pollution. These covered things like hazardous spill responses, protective clothing, port and tanker safety regulations, and pollution liability legislation.

But by far the most proposed programs fell under historic preservation, where there were seven "priority" initiatives and nine "second priority" initiatives. These included everything from an awards program and conference to lighthouse leasing to history preservation training.

FIGURE 5.8 A memorandum from staffer Jeffrey N. Shane, February 29, 1984, regarding environmental initiatives

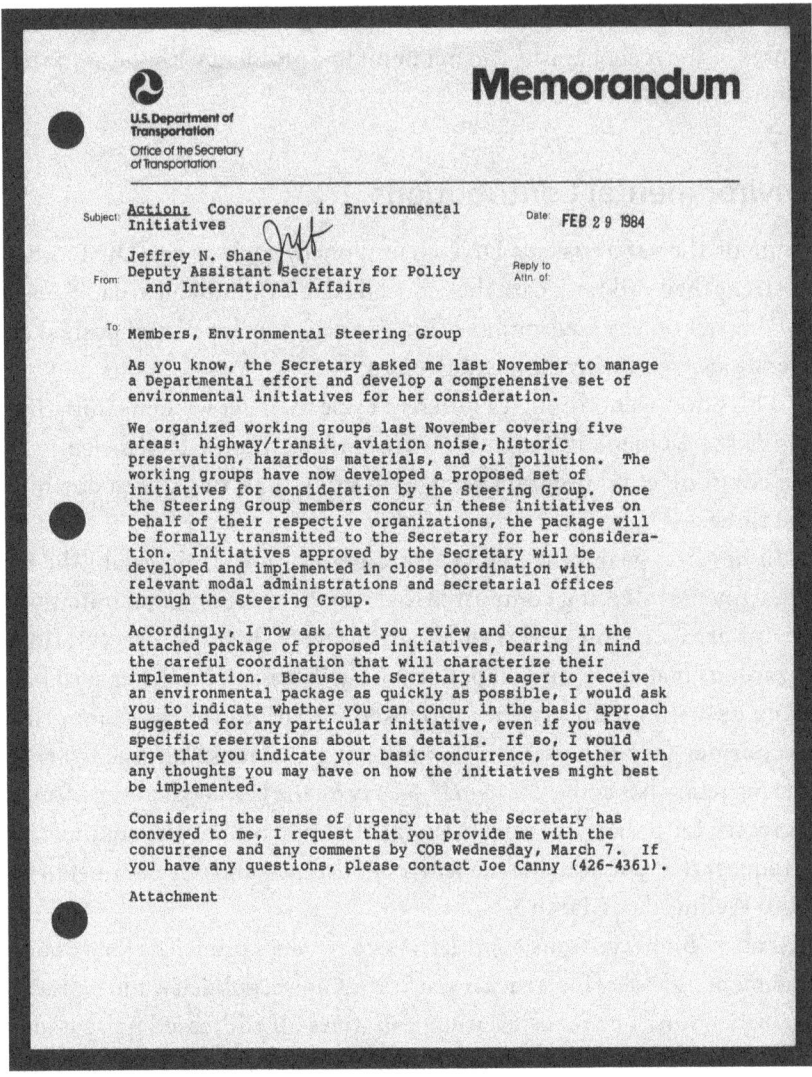

Dole blue-lined the lengthy memo with notes and questions. In June, Shane sent Dole a memo outlining the "final set of environmental initiatives" and some of the remaining concerns. Some initiatives already had been accomplished or were in the works by this time. A historic preservation awards program and conference, for instance, had been held in May

FIGURE 5.9 A memorandum from a staffer regarding the status of environmental initiatives, October 1984

OCT 16 1984

Memorandum to: The Secretary
From: Connie Heckman

For a period of months, I have taken an active role in the coordination process for the Environmental Initiatives Package submitted by Jeff Shane.

The original package was truly a mixed-bag, with proposed initiatives ranging from promotion of historic preservation efforts already underway in the Department to a recommendation to phase out the manufacture and use of Stage 2 aircraft. Many items were non-controversial, but questionable in terms of true environmental impact. Others were highly charged and require significantly more thought in terms of basic policy and timing. Still others needed only some fine-tuning or additional explanation.

In order to ease the acceptance of the less controversial items, a new package was constructed deleting the proposals which require further thought. The revised package was then returned to Jeff with the request that he review it, make any changes or updates as he saw fit and return it to S-2. Unfortunately, Jeff did not have an opportunity to review the package before it was recalled yesterday. Both the original package and the scaled down version are attached for your review.

Here are the major items which were deleted from the original package:

HAZARDOUS MATERIALS
   A new categorical grant program for training and equipment for state/local hazardous material spill prevention and clean up.

TRUCK NOISE
   Increased enforcement by BMCS of truck noise standards and a recommendation that EPA be urged to move ahead with a higher standard. It was also recommended that states be encouraged to enforce noise regulations more vigorously.

TRANSIT NOISE
   Institute a noise research and technology sharing program at an estimated cost of $200,000 to $800,000 per year for four years.

AIRPLANE NOISE
   Prohibit U.S. air carriers from purchasing newly-manufactured Stage 2 aircraft after some fixed date, possibly January, 1986.

   Prohibit existing Stage 2 aircraft from being added to the U.S. registry.

Source: The Elizabeth Dole Collection, Robert J. Dole Institute of Politics, University of Kansas

and the proposal was to make this an annual event. Also, renovations were nearly complete on San Francisco's historic cable car system.

Others, however, began to bog down in the governmental bureaucracy, and most of the original package was cut or put on the shelf (see Figure 5.9). "Many items were non-controversial, but questionable in terms of true environmental impact," according to a staffer's memorandum to Dole in October 1984. "Others were highly charged and require significantly more thought in terms of basic policy and timing. Still others needed only some fine-tuning or additional explanation" (Heckman 1984).

In an effort to "ease the acceptance," the original package was whittled down to just three items: one promoting "stronger actions to encourage preparation of noise abatement plans by airport operators," one seeking congressional approval for pollution liability reforms and a comprehensive plan for responding to oil spills, and one creating a policy statement outlining the department's existing regulatory environmental policies. "Although the contents do not break new ground," the memo said, "this statement provides explicit recognition and status for statutory and regulatory environmental policies of the Department" (Heckman 1984).

While Dole's accomplishments in these areas weren't the most dramatic, her efforts mirror a common pattern in industry today—moving from high-flying ambitions and lofty aspirations to modest levels of concreteness and statements of policy.

Leading in Leadership

When it came to leadership, Dole was in many ways well ahead of her times. Dole's sense of personal obligation to the greater good and her servant leadership style were exemplary and are highly relevant in today's work world, particularly in supply chains where many functions are a service to the business and customers.

Executive ownership of talent development (van Hoek, Gibson, and Johnson 2020; Birou and van Hoek 2021) and executive support of critical supplier relationships (Mena, van Hoek, and Christopher 2021), for example, are widely understood. While command and control was the more typical approach in Dole's days, she demonstrated the effectiveness of a more human, inclusive manner.

Dole took office as Secretary of Transportation on the heels of several significant regulatory changes to the US supply chain industry. The Airline Deregulation Act of 1978, the Motor Carrier Act of 1980, and the Staggers Rail Act of 1980 ushered in major deregulation initiatives for the airline, trucking, and rail industries, respectively. Then the Surface Transportation

Assistance Act of 1982 led trucking companies to make several operational adjustments, including the switch from cab-over-engine tractors to conventional cabs while shifting to bigger and heavier trailers.

Companies in the 1980s were figuring out how to operate effectively given these massive regulatory changes to the business landscape, all while the nation dealt with a severe recession. Dole's DOT felt the burden of developing policies and creating initiatives that would support an economic recovery and move the industry forward with a dual emphasis on safety and growth done in partnership with industry and academia in a silo-busting approach.

For instance, she regularly touted the productivity benefits of the Surface Transportation Assistance Act of 1982, which was estimated to create operating cost savings of $4.9 billion across the industry, while also funding studies for innovative ways to use the interstate system to create segments for "a special class" of "double and triple trailer" combinations. "We are extending the hand of fellowship and partnership to business, industry, academia, and labor," she said (E. Dole 1983b).

Dole often found herself winning battles that had been decades in the making. For instance, transferring federally owned airports to a regional authority had been proposed eight times since 1949 and never been voted out of committee in the House or Senate. Dole, as transportation secretary, led an effort to get that legislation passed. Thus, Dulles International Airport and the new Reagan National Airport were able to use revenue bonds, not federal taxpayer dollars, to fund growth.

She also sold Conrail, the government's freight railroad, in what at the time was the largest public offering of its kind. "You made Conrail the flagship of privatization in the United States," President Reagan (1987) told her when listing her accomplishments.

And she led the effort to reopen and redevelop the historic Union Station in Washington, DC, which had been closed for more than five years. It remains a vibrant mixed-use hub for shopping, dining, and, of course, intermodal transportation.

In addition to her diversity and inclusion efforts to address the lagging opportunities for women in transportation, Dole championed the advancement of other minorities, including the disabled.

One honor granted by the secretary at the DOT annual award ceremony, for instance, recognized employees at all levels for promoting "equal opportunity through unusually effective leadership, skill, imagination, and perseverance." Another award was specifically given to the "Outstanding Physically Handicapped Employee" (DOT1985). Her speech at the 1985 ceremony included a handwritten note to remind her to acknowledge the work the DOT was doing for women, minorities, and the disabled.

Dole recognized a shift in leadership and management that was bringing a greater emphasis on the human factor.

"We must focus on improving the management skills and the motivation of our people—with particular emphasis on getting people involved in the identification and solution of problems through a participative management approach," she said. "Herein lies our challenge. Business, government, labor and academic leaders in America can no longer maintain an attitude of indifference toward each other and toward the 'people problems' of productivity. We must have a unified effort by key segments of American society and they must address the 'people problems'" (1983c).

And, interestingly, Dole recognized that the leadership strengths that would be in high demand were not only her strengths but strengths common among women, reinforcing how a focus on diversity and inclusion makes good business and economic sense (see Figure 5.10).

"In the years ahead, executives must wake up to the fact that the very interpersonal skills of consensus building, mediating, moderating, and dealing effectively with people—skills that studies and surveys have historically identified as predominant in women—are the building blocks of a postindustrial society," she said in a 1983 speech. "It's the management of people and not the management of machinery or material that will be crucial" (1983c).

Dole recognized the value of diversity as an aspect of social sustainability for business, and she saw the emergence of women and minorities in the workforce as a "revolutionary change" in society. "I think we don't realize how significant it is because we are living it," she said (E. Dole 1986).

She pointed out that a record 19.5 million mothers with children under the age of eighteen were in the US labor force, that more than half of all American women had jobs, and that three-fifths of married couples were two-income families. More women, she noted, were entering professional careers previously dominated by men, and they were making major

FIGURE 5.10 Talking points for Secretary Dole at the Seminar for Prospective Women Managers on September 29, 1983, in Williamsburg, Virginia

3

GOOD MOTHER, GOOD-LOOKING, GOOD TEMPERED, WELL-DRESSED, WELL-GROOMED AND UNAGGRESSIVE."

* BUT WE WOMEN ARE NOT THE ONLY ONES WHO ARE CHANGING.

* IN THE YEARS AHEAD, EXECUTIVES MUST WAKE UP TO THE FACT THAT THE VERY INTERPERSONAL SKILLS OF CONSENSUS BUILDING, MEDIATING, MODERATING AND DEALING EFFECTIVELY WITH PEOPLE -- SKILLS THAT STUDIES AND SURVEYS HAVE HISTORICALLY IDENTIFIED AS PREDOMINANT IN WOMEN -- ARE THE BUILDING BLOCKS OF A POST INDUSTRIAL SOCIETY.

* IT'S THE MANAGEMENT OF PEOPLE AND NOT THE MANAGEMENT OF MACHINERY OR MATERIAL THAT WILL BE CRUCIAL.

* IT'S INTERESTING TO FLIP THROUGH THE AMERICAN MANAGEMENT ASSOCIATION'S CATALOG OF CONTINUING EDUCATION AND NOTE THE NUMBER OF COURSES IN INTERPERSONAL SKILLS BEING OFFERED TO TODAY'S MANAGERS,

Source: The Elizabeth Dole Collection, Robert J. Dole Institute of Politics, University of Kansas

contributions as blue-collar workers and as entrepreneurs. "Businesses owned by women are the fastest-growing segment of the small business community—over three million strong, as big as the population of Chicago—and generating over $53 billion in receipts," she said (1986).

In modern supply chains, where it's vital to collaborate and coordinate across functions, the people skills of participative management are highly relevant to organizational success. Automation and technology in the digital age are enabling people and augmenting work, not replacing workers, and interpersonal leadership skills are critical (WEF 2018).

This reality was driven home during the global COVID-19 pandemic and as the world began to recover and adjust in its aftermath. Many sectors were rocked by employee resignations, and managers found it more and more challenging to recruit and retain talent. In 2022, there was a renewed call for leaders to be vulnerable, show their human side, and connect with the humanity of those they were leading—all traits Dole exemplified decades ago.

Dole's leadership was seen not just in her words but in her actions. For instance, not only did she call for more training that supported the advancement of leadership, but she also showed up at training events to encourage the participants, she fought for them in high-level meetings, and she acknowledged employees who excelled by giving them public recognition.

Dole modeled the advice that leaders need to own talent development and she was passionate about creating leadership opportunities for women, of course, because she had often found herself as one of the few women leaders in arenas dominated by men. "For most women," she said in 1983, "success today still is achieved by dwelling in the improbable, by challenging the odds and overcoming the conventional wisdom" (1983a).

She often noted how she was welcomed "somewhat uneasily" into what was known as the "fellowship of educated men" when she was one of only twenty-four women in her graduating class of 550 students at Harvard Law School in 1965.[1]

"I've seen enormous progress since then," she said (1983a). "I've seen the circle expand and opportunities open up. And I am convinced that today's women stand in the reflected light of a rising, not a setting sun. Our day has barely dawned. Our dreams are just beginning to be realized. We dwell in possibility—but we challenge the improbable" (see Figure 5.11).

Today's Relevance

Heather Sheehan is former vice president of procurement and logistics for Danahar Corporation, former chair of the CSCMP board of directors, and former executive director of AWESOME, an executive-level network for advancing women in supply chain management. She was kind enough to provide her opinion on the relevance of Dole's accomplishments for today's leaders.

Sheehan told me the success of Dole's ten-point plan was particularly impressive given the challenges she faced gaining buy-in for it during that

---

1. At modern Harvard graduation ceremonies, this circle now includes "men and women" and is a distinction given to those who earn bachelor's degrees.

FIGURE 5.11 Remarks prepared for delivery by Secretary Dole to the Women's Transportation Seminar, Washington, DC, May 16, 1983

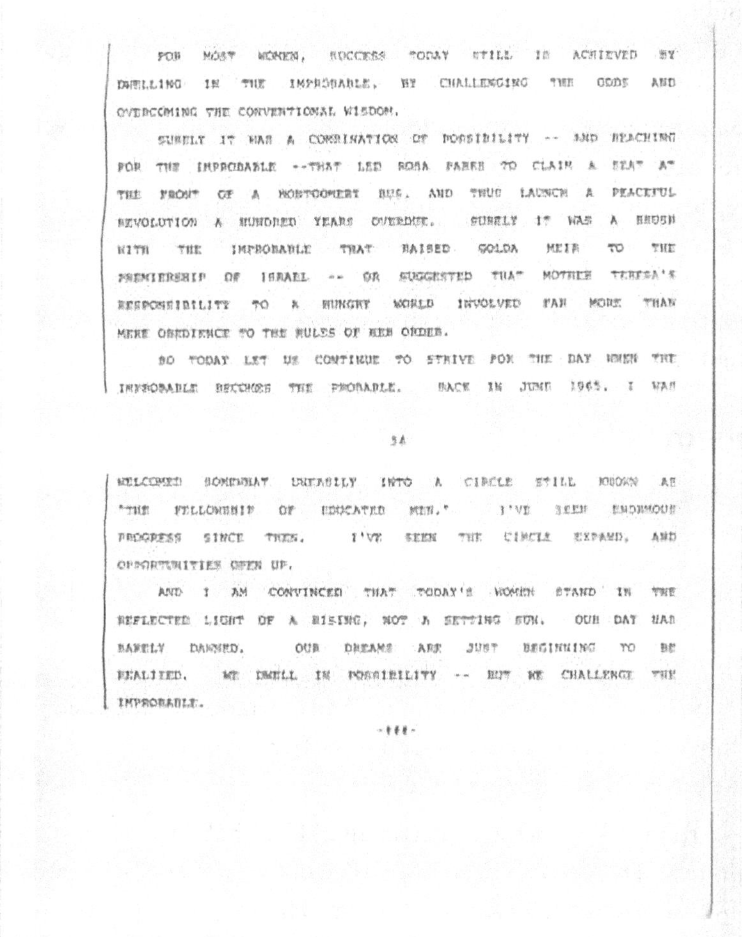

FOR MOST WOMEN, SUCCESS TODAY STILL IS ACHIEVED BY DWELLING IN THE IMPROBABLE, BY CHALLENGING THE ODDS AND OVERCOMING THE CONVENTIONAL WISDOM.

SURELY IT WAS A COMBINATION OF POSSIBILITY -- AND REACHING FOR THE IMPROBABLE --THAT LED ROSA PARKS TO CLAIM A SEAT AT THE FRONT OF A MONTGOMERY BUS, AND THUS LAUNCH A PEACEFUL REVOLUTION A HUNDRED YEARS OVERDUE. SURELY IT WAS A BRUSH WITH THE IMPROBABLE THAT RAISED GOLDA MEIR TO THE PREMIERSHIP OF ISRAEL -- OR SUGGESTED THAT MOTHER TERESA'S RESPONSIBILITY TO A HUNGRY WORLD INVOLVED FAR MORE THAN MERE OBEDIENCE TO THE RULES OF HER ORDER.

SO TODAY LET US CONTINUE TO STRIVE FOR THE DAY WHEN THE IMPROBABLE BECOMES THE PROBABLE. BACK IN JUNE 1965, I WAS

3A

WELCOMED SOMEWHAT UNEASILY INTO A CIRCLE STILL KNOWN AS "THE FELLOWSHIP OF EDUCATED MEN." I'VE SEEN ENORMOUS PROGRESS SINCE THEN. I'VE SEEN THE CIRCLE EXPAND, AND OPPORTUNITIES OPEN UP.

AND I AM CONVINCED THAT TODAY'S WOMEN STAND IN THE REFLECTED LIGHT OF A RISING, NOT A SETTING SUN. OUR DAY HAS BARELY DAWNED. OUR DREAMS ARE JUST BEGINNING TO BE REALIZED. WE DWELL IN POSSIBILITY -- BUT WE CHALLENGE THE IMPROBABLE.

-†††-

Source: The Elizabeth Dole Collection, Robert J. Dole Institute of Politics, University of Kansas

era. "The 1980s were a time where authoritarian leadership was typical, and she took a different approach to people management that is well-accepted today," said Sheehan (2022). "Also, her 10-point plan was particularly revolutionary because in the 1980s the idea of providing women with training, programs, and focus was regarded as 'special treatment' and not well-accepted. The concepts and acceptance of diversity as beneficial to organizational performance was not understood at that time."

The ten-point plan, Sheehan went on to say, was surprisingly consistent with the recommendations for supply chain diversity action that were published in the AWESOME/Gartner 2022 Women in Supply Chain Research. "Those recommendations are about driving accountability for measurable improvements in diversity, motivating and engaging women in first-line positions for training, preparation and development for higher positions, and implementing specific programs to pull more women into senior management positions," she said. "All of these are clearly part of Dole's ten-point plan. Additionally, there are opportunities to address issues of mid-career retention of women who leave their organizations over lack of advancement, compensation, lack of development and lack of flexibility" (2022).

Elizabeth Dole Timeline

1958—Elizabeth Hanford graduates Phi Beta Kappa from Duke University.

1965—Having already earned a master's degree from Harvard, Hanford completes a JD from Harvard Law School and is one of twenty-four women to graduate in the class of 550.

April 1, 1967—The US Department of Transportation, established October 15, 1966, by an act of Congress, begins operations; 18.5 percent of its workforce is female.

1973—After working in the Department of Health, Education and Welfare and for the White House Office of Consumer Affairs in the Johnson and Nixon administrations, Hanford is appointed by President Nixon to the Federal Trade Commission.

December 6, 1975—Elizabeth Hanford and Bob Dole are joined in marriage.

February 7, 1983—President Ronald Reagan appoints Dole to become the first female secretary of transportation; at that time, 19 percent of the DOT workforce is female, an increase of just 0.5 percentage point in the sixteen years since the department was established.

January 25, 1989—Dole is appointed US secretary of labor by President George H. W. Bush, making her the first woman to serve in two different cabinet positions in the administrations of two presidents.

1991–1998—Dole serves as president of the American Red Cross, the only woman to hold that position since founder Clara Barton.

2000—Dole seeks the Republican presidential nomination, becoming the first viable female candidate for a major political party.

2002—Dole is elected US senator for North Carolina, the first woman from that state to serve in the role.

Women in Transportation Timeline

In 1856, Joshua Patten, captain of the merchant clipper ship *Neptune's Car*, developed tuberculosis and collapsed into a coma near Cape Horn during a journey from New York to San Francisco.

His first mate had been confined to his cabin as punishment for sleeping on his watch. He also was suspected of sabotaging the ship's efforts to travel as fast as possible. Two other ships had set off at the same time for the same destination, and, as was the custom, wagers on which would arrive first were common. It was thought the first mate might have bet on a competitor. The second mate, meanwhile, was illiterate and unqualified to navigate.

Mary Patten, the captain's wife, was only nineteen years old, but she had spent the previous seventeen months traveling with her husband and had passed the time by learning to navigate. She surveyed the circumstances, took command of the vessel, its crew, and its cargo, and fifty-six days later brought the ship safely into San Francisco's harbor (*New York Daily Tribune* 1857).

History is full of women who made an impact in the transportation and logistics industry. Some, like Mary Patten, stepped in and took charge when opportunity presented itself, and others had more sustained involvements. Here's a look at some of the pioneers from a compilation created by the US Department of Transportation (DOT, n.d., "Timeline"):

1825—Rebecca Lukens becomes CEO of the Brandywine Iron Works, which produces iron for the boilers and hulls of ships and for railcars and rails. She is the first female CEO of a US industrial company, and she runs it until 1847.

1855—Susan Morningstar becomes one of the first women on record employed by a railroad when the Baltimore and Ohio Railroad hires her to clean, maintain, and decorate the interior of passenger cars.

1856—Mary Patten takes command of the merchant ship *Neptune's Car* when her husband, the captain, falls ill. She navigates the ship around Cape Horn and all the way to its port in San Francisco.

1870—Eliza Murfey patents sixteen devices that are used to lubricate the axles of railroad cars, reducing derailments caused by seized axles and bearings.

1877—Emily Gross is granted a patent for improvements in stone pavements.

1879—Mary Walton receives a patent for a method of deflecting smokestack emissions through water tanks to capture pollutants, which then were carried by the water through the city sewage system. She adapts the system for use on locomotives.

1889—Thea Foss founds a shipbuilding company in Tacoma, Washington, that becomes the Foss Maritime Company.

1891—Mary Walton earns a patent for a sound-dampening apparatus for elevated railways.

1901—Sarah Clark Kidder is named president of the Nevada County Narrow Gauge Railroad in California.

1903—Mary Anderson patents a window cleaning device, the predecessor of today's windshield wipers.

1910—Bessica Raiche becomes the first woman pilot in America to make a planned flight.

1911—Harriet Quimby is the first US woman to earn a pilot certificate from the France-based Federation Aeronautique Internationale (FAI). She is also the first women to fly at night and, in 1912, the first woman to pilot her own aircraft across the English Channel.

1917—Charlotte Bridgwood patents the first automatic windshield wiper.

1920—Olive Dennis becomes the first "service engineer" when the Baltimore & Ohio Railroad creates the position for her. She earns several patents, including one for the Dennis ventilator, which is inserted in the window sashes of passenger cars and controlled by passengers. She also contributes to the development of air-conditioned coaches, dimmers on overhead lights, individual reclining seats, and stain-resistant upholstery. She is the first female member of the American Railway Engineering Association.

1921—Bessie Coleman is the first African American, male or female, to earn a pilot's license from the FAI.

1922—Helen Schultz founds the first female-owned bus line, the Red Ball Transportation Company, which provides city-to-city transportation by bus across northern Iowa.

1927—At age sixteen, Elinor Smith becomes the youngest licensed pilot to date in the United States. In 1930, she becomes the youngest pilot, male or female, granted a transport license by the US Department of Commerce.

1929—Elizabeth Drennan receives a commercial truck driver's license and goes on to run Drennan Truck Line for more than twenty years.

1932—Olive Ann Beech, along with her husband Walter, cofound Beech Aircraft Company.

1934—Central Airlines hires Helen Richey as a pilot, making her the first female pilot for a US commercial airline.

1936 Louise Thaden wins the Bendix Trophy Race in the first year that women are allowed to compete, setting a new record flying from New York City to Los Angeles in 14 hours, 55 minutes. In cooperation with Frances Marsalis she also sets an endurance record, flying over Long Island for 196 hours.

1939—Willa Brown is the first African American commercial pilot and first African American woman officer in the Civil Air Patrol. She also helps establish the National Airmen's Association of America, which works to open the US Armed Forces to African American men.

1940—Frances Prothero becomes the first female manager for UPS (United Parcel Service).

1940—Mary Converse becomes the first woman to earn captain's papers (for yachts of any tonnage) in the US Merchant Marine.

During World War II, she teaches navigation to Naval Reserve officers.

1941—The Civil Aeronautics Administration begins hiring and training women to be air traffic controllers.

1942—Beatrice Alice Hicks becomes the first female engineer employed by Western Electric. She develops a crystal oscillator that generates radio frequencies, a technology used in aircraft communications. Later, while working as vice president and chief engineer at her family's Newark Controls Company, she develops environmental sensors for heating and cooling systems—NASA later used much of this technology in its space program.

1943—Helene Rother becomes the first woman to work as an automotive designer when she joins the interior styling staff of General Motors in Detroit.

1943—Janet Waterford Bragg becomes the first African American woman to earn a federal commercial pilot's license.

1943—Mazie Lanham becomes the first female driver for UPS.

1948—Marilyn Jorgenson Reece becomes the first female engineer for California's Division of Highways (now Caltrans). In 1965 she designs the I-10/405 interchange (now named after her) and later works on construction of the I-605 Freeway, the I-210 extension, and the I-105 Century Freeway.

1952—M. Gertrude Rand becomes the first female fellow of the Illuminating Society of North America. She works on the design for lighting the Holland Tunnel under the Hudson River between New York City and Jersey City, New Jersey, and develops vision standards for airplane pilots and ship lookouts during World War II.

1953—Jacqueline Cochran is the first woman to break the sound barrier.

1958—President Dwight D. Eisenhower names Mabel MacFerran Rockwell Woman Engineer of the Year for her contributions to national defense. She is one of the first woman aeronautical engineers in the United States and becomes known for demonstrating the greater effectiveness and efficiency of spot welding as opposed to riveting. She designs the guidance systems for the Polaris missile and the Atlas guided missile launcher, and she helps design the electrical installations at the Boulder and Hoover Dams. She also designs underwater propulsion systems and submarine guidance mechanisms.

1961—Dana Ulery is the first female engineer at NASA's Jet Propulsion Laboratory, developing real-time tracking systems using a North American Aviation Recomp II, a computer with a forty-bit word size.

1961—Jane Jacobs publishes *The Death and Life of Great American Cities*, one of the most influential books in the history of city planning. Her concepts of bringing life to city streets still influence pedestrian and transit planning efforts today.

1962—Beverly Cover becomes the first woman highway engineer to join the Bureau of Public Roads, the predecessor of the Federal Highway Administration.

1965—Stephanie Louise Kwolek discovers liquid crystalline polymers, which eventually leads to the development of Kevlar. Originally intended to reinforce the rubber in radial tires, Kevlar is now used for mooring cables, aircraft and space vehicle parts, sails, and bulletproof vests.

1968—Elinor Williams becomes the first female African American air traffic controller.

1968—Southern Pacific employee Leah "Rosie" Rosenfeld files and settles a sex-discrimination suit that results in changes to California's women's protective laws and opens senior positions at the railroad for women.

1971—Wally Funk becomes the first female FAA inspector and, in 1973, the first female in the FAA's System Airworthiness Analysis Program. Funk moves on to the National Transportation Safety Board (NTSB) in 1974, becoming one of the board's first female air safety investigators.

1973—Emily Howell Warner is the first woman hired as an air transport pilot for a modern, jet-equipped scheduled airline (Frontier Airlines).

1973—Bonnie Tiburzi becomes the first women pilot for a major US commercial airline (American Airlines).

1973—Santa Fe Railway hires its first female locomotive engineer, Christene Gonzales.

1977—Joan Claybrook becomes the first female administrator of the National Highway Traffic Safety Administration (NHTSA).

1977—The Women's Transportation Seminar (WTS) is founded to improve professional and personal advancement and develop industry and government recognition for women in transportation.

1980—Alinda Burke becomes the first woman deputy administrator of the Federal Highway Administration (FHWA).

1980—Candy Lightner founds Mothers Against Drunk Drivers (MADD), which grows into one of the most influential safety advocacy groups in the country.

1980—Lynn Rippelmeyer is the first woman to pilot a Boeing 747.

1982—Arlene Feldman becomes New Jersey's Director of Aeronautics, the first woman to head a state division of aeronautics. In 1984 she begins her career with the FAA as the first female deputy director of the FAA Technical Center in Atlantic City, New Jersey. In 1986 she becomes the first female deputy director of the FAA's Western Pacific Region in Los Angeles, California. She becomes the FAA's highest-ranking non-politically appointed woman in 1988 when she is named the New England Regional Administrator. In 1994, she becomes the director of FAA's Eastern Region.

1983—Carmen Turner becomes the general manager of the Washington Metropolitan Area Transit Authority (WMATA). She is the first African American woman to lead a major transit agency.

1983—Elizabeth Hanford Dole is sworn in as the first woman secretary of the Department of Transportation.

1983—Sally Ride becomes the first US woman in space.

1984—Beverly Burns is the first woman to captain a Boeing 747 cross country.

1988—Arlene Westermeyer becomes UPS's first female pilot.

1988—Barbara McConnell Barrett becomes FAA's first female deputy administrator.

1988—Christine Owens becomes the first woman district manager for UPS.

1993—Sheila Widnall is appointed as the first female secretary of the Air Force, holding that office until 1997. She holds three patents on airflow technology and is recognized for her contributions to fluid mechanics, specifically in the areas of aircraft turbulence and spiraling airflows called vortices.

1993—Jolene Molitoris becomes the first woman to head the Federal Railroad Administration.

1994—*Engineering News-Record* selects Ginger Evan, a civil engineer, as the first woman to receive its "Man of the Year Award" for her work overseeing the construction of the Denver International Airport. The award is now called the "Award of Excellence and Woman of the Year."

1995—Lea Soupata becomes the first woman to serve on UPS's Management Committee.

1997—Ann Livermore becomes the first woman to serve on the UPS board of directors.

1997—Jane Garvey becomes the first woman administrator of the FAA and the first administrator to serve a five-year term.

1997—The League of Railway Industry Women forms to provide leadership and support for the personal and professional growth of women at every level in railroading and railway-related businesses.

1999—Lt. Col. Eileen Collins serves as NASA's first female space shuttle commander.

2000—Rodica Baranescu, Ph.D., becomes the first woman president of the Society of Automotive Engineers. As an engineer at the International Truck and Engine Corporation she works on developing environmentally friendly fuel, lubricants, and coolants for diesel engines.

2012—The American Road and Transportation Builders Association's Transportation Development Foundation awards the Ethel S. Birchland Lifetime Achievement Award to Katie Turnbull for her thirty-five years of work in transportation, research, service, and education. Turnbull is a recognized expert on high-occupancy vehicle facilities, toll facilities, managed lanes, public transportation,

transportation planning, travel demand management, and intelligent transportation systems.

2012—Sue Cischke retires after thirty-five years of service in the automobile industry. She leaves the industry after serving as Ford's vice president of sustainability, environment and safety engineering since 2008. Before joining Ford in 2001, she was senior vice president of regulatory affairs and passenger car operations for DaimlerChrysler. She began her career at Chrysler Corporation in 1976.

2012—Ann Drake, chairman and CEO of DSC Logistics, becomes the first woman to receive CSCMP's Distinguished Service Award, which recognized her as a "tireless advocate for the importance of the supply chain and a visible example of using logistics to drive performance, growth, and manage change." Ann goes on to found AWESOME, a nonprofit focused on advancing more women into senior leadership in supply chain management, and she is now developing a separate women's leadership center.

2012—Ilya Espino de Marotta is named the first female executive vice president of engineering for the Panama Canal Authority, and then leads the major expansion of the canal that opened in 2016. She has since been named deputy administrator of the canal with responsibility for all of its operations.

References

Birou, L. and R. van Hoek. 2021. "Supply Chain Management Talent: The Role of Executives in Engagement, Recruitment, Development and Retention," *Supply Chain Management* 27, no. 6, 712–727.

Dole, B. 2010. *Tributes Delivered in Congress to Elizabeth Dole.* S. Doc. No. 110-22, at 13-19. US Government Printing Office, Washington, 2010.

Dole, E. 1983a. Remarks prepared for delivery by Secretary Elizabeth Hanford Dole to the Woman's Transportation Seminar, Washington, DC, May 16, 1983, Elizabeth Dole Collection, box 36, folder 4, Robert and Elizabeth Dole Archive and Special Collections, Robert J. Dole Institute of Politics, University of Kansas, Lawrence, Kansas.

Dole, E. 1983b. Remarks prepared for delivery by Secretary Elizabeth Hanford Dole, White House conference on productivity, session on government organization and operations, September 23, 1983, Elizabeth Dole Collection, box 40, folder 1.

Dole, E. 1983c. Typed speaking notes, September 29, 1983, Williamsburg, Virginia, Seminar for Prospective Women Managers. Elizabeth Dole Collection, box 40, folder 3.

Dole, E. 1983d. Remarks prepared for delivery by Secretary Elizabeth Hanford Dole to the American Association of State Highway and Transportation Officials, Denver, Colorado, October 3, 1983. Elizabeth Dole Collection.

Dole, E. 1984a. Remarks prepared for delivery by Secretary of Transportation Elizabeth Hanford Dole, Women's Business Ownership Conference 1984, Orlando, Florida, June 9, 1984. Elizabeth Dole Collection.

Dole, E. 1984b. Department of Transportation Federal Women's Week, Washington, DC, October 23, 1984. Elizabeth Dole Collection, box 53, folder 9.

Dole, E. 1985a. Notes for Executive Women's Briefing, August 8, 1985. Elizabeth Dole Collection, box 8, folder 8.

Dole, E. 1985b. Statement by Secretary of Transportation Elizabeth Hanford Dole, press conference, September 19, 1985. Elizabeth Dole Collection, box 1, folder 9.

Dole, E. 1986. Remarks prepared for delivery by Secretary of Transportation Elizabeth Hanford Dole to the Fourth Annual Conference on Women, April 14, 1986, Anaheim, California. Elizabeth Dole Collection, box 65, folder 9.

Domestic Policy Council. 1985. Minutes, September 19. Elizabeth Dole Collection, box 1, folder 9.

DOT (Department of Transportation). 1985. The Secretary's 18th Annual Awards Program, October 17, 1985, Elizabeth Dole Collection, box 5, folder 9.

DOT. n.d. "The Secretary of Transportation's Initiative to Improve Opportunities for Women," Elizabeth Dole Collection, e-dot_006-001_001. (While there is no date on this brochure, it most likely was published in the first half of 1983.)

DOT. n.d. "Timeline of Women in Transportation History." Accessed February 10, 2022. https://www.transportation.gov/womenandgirls/timeline/accessible.

Heckman, Connie. 1984. Memorandum, October 6. Elizabeth Dole Collection, box 27, folder 3.

Hoek, R. van, B. Gibson, and M. Johnson. 2020. "Talent Management for a Post-COVID-19 Supply Chain: The Critical Role for Managers." *Journal of Business Logistics* 41, no. 4, 334–336.

Mena, C., R. van Hoek, and M. Christopher. 2021. *Leading Procurement Strategy*. London: Kogan Page.

National Safety Council. n.d. "The National Safety Council Recognizes the Honorable Elizabeth Dole: Celebrating a Lifetime of Lifesaving Contribution and Service to Safety." https://www.nsc.org/getmedia/fba1469d-a19e-4abf-8cd9-1136cb7da7e7/elizabeth-dole-accomplishments.pdf.aspx.

New York Daily Tribune. 1857. "A Heroine of the Sea," February 18.

Plymate, Debra L. n.d. Letter to Elizabeth Dole. Elizabeth Dole Collection, box 5, folder 9.

Rainey, J. 2007. "Elizabeth Dole Interview Transcript" from "A Few Good Women Oral History collection," created by Barbara Hackman Franklin. Penn State University Libraries, State College, Pennsylvania. https://libraries.psu.edu/about/collections/few-good-women/biographies/elizabeth-dole/elizabeth-dole-interview-transcript.

Reagan, R. 1987. Letter to Elizabeth Dole, September 14. Elizabeth Dole Collection, box 3, folder 9.

Shane, J. 1984. Memorandum, February 29. Elizabeth Dole Collection, box 27, folder 3.

Sheehan, Heather. 2022. E-mail message to author, June 1.

US Congress. 1986. Commercial Motor Vehicle Safety Act of 1986, S. 1903. 99th Cong., 1985–1986.

World Economic Forum. 2018. *The Future of Jobs Report*. Geneva: World Economic Forum.

Johnnie Bryan (J. B.) Hunt

Birth: February 28, 1927
Died: December 7, 2006 (age 79)
Company: J.B. Hunt Transport Services
Hall of Fame Induction: 2016
Key Supply Chain Innovation: Pioneer of intermodal partnerships between trucking and railroads

Johnnie Bryan Hunt began his journey into supply chain innovation on the front lines of the industry. Make that the front seat.

Hunt was selected to the CSCMP Supply Chain Hall of Fame primarily for his contribution to modern intermodal logistics—the partnership he helped create in 1989 between his trucking company and the Santa Fe Railway that changed how products are moved across America and around the world.

To understand why he would go all-in on what many experts in trucking and railway at the time considered an almost laughable venture, however, you have to understand Hunt's hardscrabble background and the inspiration he found in the days when he drove trucks rather than owned them.

Growing up in rural north-central Arkansas during the Great Depression, Hunt followed in his father's footsteps by working long hours to help support the family. He dropped out of school after the seventh grade and took whatever work he could, mostly toiling for long hours at his uncle's sawmill. It was there that he began driving trucks (Thompson and Waller 2019).

When he turned eighteen in 1945, he joined the US Army, but he declined an opportunity to attend officers' training school at the end of World War II and returned home to Heber Springs, Arkansas, in 1947 (Schwartz 1992). Hunt went back to the mill and back to driving a truck, but now he was old enough to haul and sell finished lumber in Arkansas, Missouri, and as far away as Illinois. And when he wasn't hauling lumber, he hauled live chickens to a processing plant in Missouri (Schwartz 1992).

Then in 1948, after a brief stint in the auction business left him $3,600 in debt, Hunt borrowed ten dollars from a friend, hitchhiked to Little Rock, and took a job as a driver for East Texas Motor Freight (Schwartz 1992). In 1952, he married Johnelle DeBusk, the daughter of a prominent merchant back in Heber Springs (Figure 6.1), and she, as the more educated of the two, would become not only his partner at home but a critical player in their shared business ventures.

Throughout most of the 1950s, however, Johnelle stayed home as they began a family, and Hunt spent most of his days and many of his nights driving across middle America for East Texas Motor Freight and, later, Superior Forwarding (Schwartz 1992).

The hours behind the wheel of a truck gave Hunt time to think—to dream the big dreams that became as much a part of his life as his cowboy

FIGURE 6.1 Johnelle and J. B. Hunt at their wedding in 1952

Source: J. B. and Johnelle Hunt Family

boots and his Stetson hat. Hunt looked through the windshield and saw the traffic on the road and the fields, hills, and cities around him, but he also focused on opportunities for his future. Hidden from others in the scenery, he saw the "what-ifs" of life and typically pursued them.

What if I sold cement when I'm not driving?

Or sod?

What if . . . ?

It was that what-if mentality that changed the course of Hunt's career and, eventually, changed the face of logistics transportation. As Hunt was driving past the rice fields near Stuttgart, Arkansas, in the late 1950s, he noticed that farmers typically burned rice hulls in the fields. The hulls that made it to the mills were gathered and hauled away to be destroyed. Hunt recognized that what rice farmers and mill owners saw as processing waste, chicken farmers could use as a base for litter for their poultry houses.

Hunt's first significant innovation, therefore, had nothing to do with trucks but everything to do with packing and hauling rice hulls. The reason no one at the time sold the hulls to poultry farmers was because there was no way to pack the fluffy hulls so they could be economically transported.

Hunt had been toying with ideas for a machine that would package wood shavings since his days at the sawmill, and his trips through Stuttgart energized him to take that idea and apply it to rice-hull packing. Soon he completed a working machine, and, with an investment of $5,533 from Winthrop Rockefeller's Winrock Enterprises and shares in the business sold mostly to poultry farmers, the J.B. Hunt Company was incorporated in 1961 (Schwartz 1992).

"The first year we were in business, we lost $19,000," Johnelle Hunt said in a 2016 video. "And all the accountants and all the people we were working with were saying you'll have to close the doors. You can't go on. . . . We had to make this work. We just kept going. We just kept working" (JBHT 2016).

The company turned a profit in its second year, and Hunt never went back to driving a truck as his primary source of income. It was 1969, however, before he bought five refrigerated trucks and began dabbling in the trucking business. And throughout the 1970s, despite fierce competition from legacy companies in the heavily regulated industry, he expanded that part of the business (see Figure 6.2).

By 1983, three years after the Motor Carrier Act of 1980 deregulated the trucking industry, the Hunts owned more than five hundred tractors and more than a thousand trailers, and the trucking operation was earning $63 million in revenue (Bentley 2013). That same year, Hunt sold the rice-hull operation in Stuttgart to Eli Lilly for $2 million and took J.B. Hunt Transport (JBHT) public (Thompson and Waller 2019).

Today it's one of the largest, most successful freight transportation companies in the world. And while it began by selling rice hulls and grew by hauling freight on the highways, it also owes much of its success to a handshake commitment during a train ride from Chicago to Kansas City.

An Intermodal Innovation

Like many of the great innovations in supply chain, coming up with a great idea is only one step in the process. It's an important one, to be

FIGURE 6.2. Johnelle and J. B. Hunt in front of truck

Photo by Richard Berquist/Berquist & Associates Photography

Source: J. B. and Johnelle Hunt Family

sure, but one could argue it's not nearly as vital as all the steps that turn the idea into a reality.

J. B. Hunt didn't come up with the idea of forming a partnership with the Santa Fe Railway to build a unique intermodal business, but he did two things that were key to making the venture a success. First, he said "yes" to the idea. Second, he put his money where his mouth was and backed the idea in ways that made other truckers laugh in the beginning and later cry with envy.

The idea itself came from Mike Haverty, the president of the Santa Fe. Haverty was on one of his trains as it rolled across a particularly rural stretch of America, and he was watching the traffic on the nearby interstate highway. It made no economic sense to him that so many trailers were being pulled individually by a truck when one of his locomotives could haul more than two hundred of them at a time. There had to be a way, he decided, to increase the intermodal option in the supply chain.

This type of transportation model was nothing new. Intermodal simply means to move freight using multiple modes—a box hauled by a horse-drawn wagon and then loaded on a barge for a trip down a river and then unloaded onto another wagon for final delivery, for instance.

In the early 1950s Malcolm McLean, another Supply Chain Hall of Famer, began working with maritime shippers, railroads, and truckers on common standards for containers. Then in 1977 he partnered with the Southern Pacific Railroad to create and test the first double-stacked intermodal rail car.

Trains like those run by Haverty, meanwhile, commonly carried freight in containers that were taken to and from the railyards by trucks. Railroad companies, however, had no part in the drayage—the short-distance hauls that were handled by a wide variety of trucking companies and that typically were arranged by third-party brokers.

Partnering with a trucking company that could manage customer relationships, market the service, and handle pickups and deliveries could provide a much-needed economic booster shot for his railway, Haverty realized. But there was just one problem: railroads and truckers were fierce competitors.

Trucking companies saw no reason to encourage intermodal because it took freight off their trucks and, consequently, money out of their pockets. And when lobbyists from the trucking industry went to the government seeking regulatory changes, the stiffest opposition typically came from the railroad industry. If truckers were the Hatfields, the railroaders were the McCoys.

Kirk Thompson, who began working for Hunt as a bookkeeper in 1973 and rose to serve as CEO from 1987 to 2011, pointed out that deregulation in 1980 only increased the railroad industry's fears and concerns that over-the-road trucks would cut into their business. "Truckers, meanwhile, wanted changes that benefited them, not rail," Thompson, who retired in 2024 as executive chairman of the JBHT board, wrote in the 2019 book he coauthored about the company's growth. "We wanted trailers with more cubic capacity, for instance, and we wanted to haul heavier loads. The industries were antagonistic, to say the least" (Thompson and Waller 2019).

Brokers emerged as go-betweens who could work out deals that kept the railroads in one corner and the trucking companies in another. That became the status quo until a consultant approached Thompson in 1989 with the idea of partnering with the Santa Fe. Thompson immediately agreed to join the discussion and took the offer to J. B. Hunt, who was chairman of the company's board.

While J.B. Hunt Transport had become one of the biggest trucking companies in America, the competition within the industry was fierce, both for drivers and for freight. The founder and the rest of the JBHT leadership team quickly saw the business sense of using fewer drivers and spending less money on the long-haul portions of their business. And they realized the right type of partnership would give them a competitive advantage over trucking companies that were married to the status quo.

Paul Bergant, who would become president of Hunt's intermodal segment, said JBHT was one of the few trucking companies that would have entertained such an idea. "If he'd made that pitch to any other trucker in the world at that time, they'd have said, 'Thank you, but no thank you' and sent him back to Chicago," Bergant said. "For us, a light bulb went on. We talked about it. We knew our model was going to be under some strain. We had to do something to change, or the outcome would be stagnation" (Thompson and Waller 2019).

The key meeting came when Hunt and his team went to Chicago for a convention and then joined Haverty and his team on a business car of one of his trains bound for Kansas City. The purpose of the trip was twofold: One, to show that the ride was smooth enough to carry freight with minimal damage, especially when it passed through the railyards. Two, so that Haverty and Hunt could talk business eye to eye in a less formal setting.

During that trip, the two titans agreed to make the partnership happen. "J. B. walked over to me and said, 'Haverty, we've got a deal,'" Haverty would later say. "I said, 'What's the deal?' He said, 'I don't know, but we're going to do it'" (Hurt 2016).

The legal contracts came later, but the deal was done. "Those two being who they were," said Bergant, "a handshake was as good as anything" (Thompson and Waller 2019).

This was a turning point for both the railroad and J.B. Hunt Transport, according to many experts, including Andy Petery, an analyst at Morgan Stanley who specialized in the railroad industry. "J. B. Hunt, the man and the company, recognized that the future was in partnering with the enemy, so to speak," Petery said. "The enemy was the railroad. If they did it successfully, they would not only enable the railroad to compete in the trucking environment, which was 75 percent of the freight business, but J.B. Hunt the company would also expand its growth prospects by using the railroads as partners and entering markets they couldn't possibly do on their own" (Thompson and Waller 2019).

By December 1989, a "strategic alliance" was announced to operate a business known as Quantum (Jouzaitis 1989). The initial route, which launched on February 5, 1990, with 150 trailers, carried containers primarily between Chicago and Los Angeles. J.B. Hunt Transport handled just about everything other than the long-haul over the rails, and the companies came up with a matrix for splitting the revenues. Soon, JBHT's entire fleet of 10,000 trailers was available for intermodal and the company had signed long-term agreements with Burlington Northern (to the Pacific Northwest) and Conrail (to the East Coast).

Those agreements have survived multiple mergers in the railroad industry, keeping JBHT at the top of the intermodal business for decades. In fact, more than thirty years after the alliance was formed, J.B. Hunt Intermodal still operated the largest fleet of company-owned fifty-three-foot containers and drayage fleets in North America. The company has partnerships with BNSF (Burlington Northern Santa Fe), Norfolk

Southern, CSX Transportation, the Canadian National Railway, and Kansas City Southern/Kansas City Southern in Mexico.

"This segment of our business represents something more than just a monumental success story—although it certainly is that," Thompson would say. "It also represents an approach to business that made J.B. Hunt Transport prosperous from the beginning and still factors into our growth and long-term success" (Thompson and Waller 2019).

The partnership itself was innovative because until then no trucking companies were collaborating with a rival railroad company. But the real genius came in the way it was set up, because those details and the heavy investment on the part of JBHT created barriers to entry that made it difficult, if not impossible, for competitors to catch up once they realized that they should, in fact, forge similar partnerships (see Figure 6.3).

J.B. Hunt Transport, for instance, had priority in the railyards, including its own gate to go in and out of the railroad terminals. The Santa Fe also agreed to modify its well cars for the containers JBHT had built.

FIGURE 6.3 Image showing intermodal

Source: J. B. and Johnelle Hunt Family

JBHT, in fact, invested millions of dollars in customized 53-foot containers that could better withstand the loading and unloading process that came with intermodal. Not only did this provide more protection for the freight, but unlike other trailers and most other containers, they could be double stacked in the train's well cars. And the company designed those containers to fit on customized chassis so that no other trucking companies could use them.

Costs decreased because JBHT created assets that were specifically used for intermodal, developed business processes specific to intermodal that, among other things, reduced empty legs, and learned from the experience that came from being first. "We developed more experience than any other carrier with full-load intermodal, hence our fixed costs associated with switching between modes steadily decreased, which created a competitive advantage," Thompson said (Thompson and Waller 2019).

One of the biggest challenges was convincing traditional truckload customers that intermodal was a better option. But they soon saw the economic benefits of using trains for longer hauls and for cutting out the fees that came with brokers.

Intermodal also proved to be a win for companies that were increasingly interested in being environmentally friendly. One train can carry the same amount of freight as hundreds of trucks, so moving more freight shipments from truck to rail reduces highway congestion and can reduce greenhouse gas emissions by up to 75 percent (AAR 2021).

In 2015, the Congressional Budget Office released a report showing that it cost 5.1 cents per ton-mile to move cargo by rail and 15.6 cents per ton-mile to move it by truck. And unpriced external costs, including the costs from pavement damage, traffic congestion, and emissions, also were found to be much higher for trucks ($2.62–$5.86 per ton-mile) than for rail ($0.30–$0.82 per ton-mile) (Austin 2015).

Craig Harper, JBHT's recently retired chief sustainability officer, pointed out that intermodal is "2.5 times more efficient" than transporting the same load just by truck. "There are very few things you can do to get that kind of step change in the amount of CO_2 emissions you generate," he told *Investor's Business Daily*, which ranked the company No. 4 on its Best ESG Companies list for 2021, behind only Microsoft,

Linde, and Accenture, and intermodal played a big role in the ranking (Doler 2021). The next year, JBHT moved up to No. 2 on the IBD list (Doler 2022).

JBHT now has more than one hundred thousand intermodal containers, and intermodal accounted for more than 60 percent of the company's 2020 operating income. "Plus, we believe that there are 7 to 11 million shipments that can be converted to intermodal," Harper said, "and you don't have to wait for any kind of innovation to take advantage of that conversion" (Doler 2021).

The intermodal partnership also created a competitive advantage over the brokers that traditionally had managed this type of business. Brokers owned almost no assets—no containers and no trucks. They served as go-betweens that arranged for freight to get from point A to point B. JBHT had its own equipment, its own drivers, and better access into and out of the railyards. It operated with greater efficiencies, lower cost, and more consistency than brokers could offer.

Very few truckload companies followed JBHT into the intermodal business, partly because they feared that it would hurt their trucking business but also because of the financial barriers to entry. Hunt's ability to see a different future and invest in it while others were content with business as usual breathed new life into his company and the railroads, while providing shippers with a cost-effective, more environmentally friendly way to move their freight.

Hunt's Principles Exemplified

There's no denying that J. B. Hunt enjoyed trying new things as a businessman, but his big ideas, even those that didn't work out, were based on some principles common to almost all supply chain innovation.

Hunt built his business around ideas that added value—to his customers, to the world, to his employees, and, of course, to his company. Most notably, Hunt created a culture that was and is willing to embrace creative disruption but that also is committed to staying connected to the company's core values and its core offerings.

John Roberts, who joined the company as a management trainee straight out of college in 1989 and became its CEO in 2011, said playing it safe is the biggest risk JBHT could ever take. "If we get too attached or too enamored of our businesses," he said, "then [the competition] will kill us, because somebody out there is going to disrupt" (Thompson and Waller 2019).

Here are a few ways the company supports an innovative culture:

Support from the top.

Thompson points out that leaders often say they want innovation but "dive for cover" when things don't go well. They are quick to pull the plug on ideas that don't show immediate promise, they fire people, and they blame everyone but themselves when something doesn't work out. JBHT as a company has learned from its founders to chase dreams with a long-term perspective, even if that means missing short-term numbers (Thompson and Waller 2019).

Value grace.

Like any good supply chain company, JBHT creates efficiencies by developing standardized processes. Improving those processes, however, requires a willingness by employees to own their work and take risks that may or may not always work out. The response by leadership to those who disrupt the status quo—and especially to the mistakes made along the way—goes a long way toward feeding or starving future ideas. Hunt, according to former long-time human resources director Mark Greenway, built a culture that gives grace for mistakes.

"Nobody plays a perfect game," Greenway said. "You're going to make a mistake. Just own it, have integrity, and don't make the same mistake over and over. So, we have developed this culture that adapts well to change. If you don't like change, don't come to J.B. Hunt. You know it's okay to make a mistake. And when you miss a tackle, you're going to get corrected and go back into the game" (Thompson and Waller 2019).

Take measured risks.

When JBHT launched its intermodal partnership with the Santa Fe, the trucking company was making very few runs from Chicago to California. In other words, the partnership wasn't just a different way to move shipments for existing customers; it was a way to bring in new customers that were shipping with competitors. The cost/benefit of the partnership, therefore, made it an attractive deal, because he could increase business in that lane without immediately hurting other areas of his business.

Plus, there was a shortage of long-haul drivers at the time, so Hunt knew the company's future rested more with shorter runs. Rather than scrambling to find drivers who were willing to cover two thousand miles of asphalt each way, he now could focus more on hiring drivers who could make deliveries and, in many cases, be home for dinner with their family.

As the intermodal venture experienced success, Hunt also was in a better position to invest and expand those operations, let go of businesses that weren't hitting financial goals, and explore new ideas like managing fleets for shippers or operating its own sophisticated brokerage division.

What is good for business can be very good for the environment.

The transportation industry is often seen as a key driver behind environmental challenges, but intermodal takes trucks off the road. While intermodal started for JBHT as a businesscentric innovation, the positive environmental implications were massive and continue to be to this day. This offers a case in point that what is good for business can be very good for the environment.

Innovation from looking at problems differently not only resulted in unexpected benefits for the environment, but also set JBHT up to become an industry leader in pursuing other innovations that were more intentionally focused on ESG goals.

JBHT also is investing in electric and hydrogen fuel cell trucks, while developing technology that plans routes more efficiently and thereby reduces the miles a truck travels empty while going to pick up a load (JBHT 2020).

JBHT also developed two proprietary tools that help "customers toward our goal to support sustainable supply chains"—the Carbon Diet service and the CLEAN Transport carbon calculator (JBHT 2020).

The Carbon Diet is built around five best practices: Know your carbon footprint as a starting point, eliminate miles, increase payload, convert to energy-efficient modes, and use efficient carriers (JBHT 2020).

The carbon calculator, meanwhile, calculates the carbon footprint of shipments so JBHT and its customers can coordinate on ways to reduce that footprint. For example, the tool can use a customer's historical data to estimate the carbon reduction that would result from using intermodal rather than over-the-road trucks (JBHT 2020).

Links to Other Supply Chain Innovators

The connections between J. B. Hunt and other supply chain innovators are varied and numerous.

Making learning and failure safe, for instance, are values that J. B. Hunt shared with Henry Ford, who did the same thing in the development of the Ford production system. And grace is a value embodied by Elizabeth Dole's focus on developing, stewarding, and promoting diverse parts of the transportation talent market.

Fellow CSCMP Supply Chain Hall of Famer Malcolm McLean was friends with J. B. Hunt, and their respective innovations complemented each other. Standardized containerization was key for intermodal, and intermodal made the benefit of containerization go much further.

Intermodal also brought together complementary technologies and elements of the transportation system, just as George Stephenson did during the creation of the modern railway system.

Today's Relevance

Intermodal remains one of the most cost-effective, environmentally friendly ways to move large shipments of goods over long distances, which is why companies continue to invest in the infrastructure that supports it.

The Association of American Railroads, for instance, points to upgrades at sites like California's Port of Long Beach's Middle

Harbor Terminal Redevelopment project as examples of the industry's commitment to intermodal. The terminal is adding on-dock rail with plans for accommodating up to 2,100 trains by 2025.

BNSF Railway, meanwhile, opened a new intermodal terminal in Kansas in 2013. "Five wide-span cranes, that produce zero emissions, transfer containers to and from trains," an article on the AAR's website said, "allowing the facility to handle up to 500,000 intermodal units a year" (2020). And the Kansas City Southern Railway Company (KCS) invested more than $64 million in a new intermodal terminal in Texas that has "modern technology, such as automated gates, optical scanners and biometric identification," that allows KCS to "quickly, efficiently and safely move hundreds of thousands of containers a year" (AAR 2020).

In addition to the environmental benefit of taking containers off the road and putting them on trains, an added benefit of intermodal is that it reduces pressure on the market for drivers, which is very tight due to a shortage of drivers.

What's Next

The legacy of J. B. Hunt when it comes to the supply chain industry might be less about the famed intermodal partnership and more about the pattern of innovation.

The company, for instance, has invested in the future of supply chain management in a number of ways through its partnerships with the University of Arkansas. Johnelle Hunt and her business partners were critical donors to and supporters of the CSCMP Hall of Fame, and the company regularly partners with the Sam M. Walton College of Business on research and teaching initiatives.

In addition to investments in students and industry research, the company continues to reinvent the way it does business. Hunt always had an eye toward the future and, despite his lack of a formal education, took an early interest in a future where information, not trucks or trains or other assets, would be a competitive advantage.

When analyst John Larkin visited Arkansas in the 1980s, Hunt drove him around the area on a tour that included pastures covered with cattle and ended up at the construction site for what's now JBHT's headquarters in Lowell, Arkansas. Hunt beamed with pride when he showed Larkin the area that would become the computer room.

"He said, 'Right here in this room, every truckload transaction that takes place in America will be processed by our computers,'" Larkin said. "He was saying they were going to be the truckload broker for the whole industry. That never totally took place, but certainly the asset-light truck brokerage concept has gotten to be a fairly big operation. And they're not done growing that part of the business" (Thompson and Waller 2019).

The "asset-light" concept has become the future of JBHT and, in many ways, the freight-hauling business as a whole. JBHT hired Stuart Scott as executive vice president and chief information officer in 2016, and the company began a rapid investment in a new approach to technology. Rather than using technology primarily to serve its internal team, Scott launched a plan to use it in far more external ways.

The company backed him, and JBHT began developing software and systems that drivers and customers, who all have access to technology on multiple devices, could use to manage their freight transportation needs. With a marketplace platform online, ecommerce has become as big a part of the JBHT business model as containers and tractors (see Figure 6.4).

Thompson describes a "glow" around JBHT that tells you it "no longer is just a company that moves freight; this is a company that makes freight move. It tells you this is no longer just a company driven by men and women in truck cabs; it's a company driven by big data and insights. It tells you, as Chief Information Officer Stuart Scott likes to put it, this no longer is an assets company that uses technology; it's a technology company that uses assets. It tells you the magic of this company isn't found in the obvious, it's found in a unique culture that consistently develops innovative and disruptive ideas—ideas that have taken JBHT from an ordinary player in an overcrowded field and turned it into a one-of-a-kind success story" (Thompson and Waller 2019).

That glow began with J. B. Hunt, and it lives on in the people who shepherd his legacy.

FIGURE 6.4 Image showing commitment to high-tech intermodal

Source: J. B. and Johnelle Hunt Family

J. B. Hunt Timeline

1961—The J.B. Hunt Company is incorporated on August 10 as an agricultural supply and rice-hull packing business. In its first year, the business loses $19,123 on revenues of $50,626.

1962—The company's rice-hull packing plant opens in Stuttgart, Arkansas, at a cost of $100,000.

1969—The J.B. Hunt Company reports revenue of $827,198 and profit of $51,550, making it the largest rice-hull dealer in the nation. It also purchases five used trucks and seven used refrigerated trailers, marking its start in the trucking industry.

1978—J.B. Hunt Transport (JBHT) acquires E.L. Reddish Transportation, adding twenty-four trucks to its fleet and expanding its services into thirty-three states.

1979—JBHT gets 90 percent of its applications to haul freight approved and begins service to the West Coast. Revenues are $14.7 million and net income is $564,000.

1980—The Federal Motor Carrier Act of 1980 deregulates the trucking industry, allowing JBHT to obtain unlimited authority to carry general commodities throughout the forty-eight contiguous states.

1983—J. B. Hunt sells his rice-hull operation in Stuttgart, Arkansas, to Eli Lilly for $2 million.

1983—J. B. Hunt takes his company public. The initial public offering results in 1.32 million shares sold, priced at $18.75 a share, and net proceeds of $18.5 million.

1988—JBHT receives Canadian authority to ship.

1989—JBHT provides transportation services to and from Mexico. Hunt also agrees to a "strategic alliance" with the Santa Fe Railway Company, the first successful venture in intermodal transportation between the rival industries.

1990—JBHT moves into a 150,000-square-foot headquarters building.

1991—JBHT begins flatbed and special commodities operations.

1992—JBHT announces a joint venture with Transportacion Maritima Mexicana (TMM), the largest transportation company in Mexico.

It also acquires a small hazardous waste carrier and begins offering transportation logistics services and dedicated contract services.

1993—JBHT expands joint truck and rail transportation in Canada with Canadian National Railroad.

1995—J. B. Hunt retires from the trucking business but remains on the company's board as "senior chairman."

1996—To concentrate on its dry van, logistics, and dedicated contract units, JBHT sells off its parcel and hazardous waste businesses. It also builds a new terminal and maintenance facility in Chicago.

1999—JBHT builds a new terminal and maintenance facility in Kansas City, Missouri.

2000—JBHT ends its logistics division. It also forms Transplace Inc. with five other companies; it owns 27 percent of the venture.

2002—JBHT ends joint venture in Mexico; sells interest in Mexico to TMM.

2004—J. B. Hunt steps down from the company board.

2006—J. B. Hunt passes away on December 7, five days after falling on ice and suffering a head injury. He was 79.

References

AAR (Association of American Railroads). 2020. "Preparing for the Future with Intermodal Freight Rail." https://www.aar.org/article/preparing-future-intermodal-freight-rail/.

AAR 2021. "Freight Railroads & Climate Change Policies." https://www.aar.org/wp-content/uploads/2021/02/AAR-Freight-Rail-Climate-Change-Fact-Sheet.pdf.

Austin, D. 2015. "Pricing Freight Transport to Account for External Costs." Working Paper 2015-03, Congressional Budget Office. https://www.cbo.gov/sites/default/files/114th-congress-2015-2016/workingpaper/50049-Freight_Transport_Working_Paper-2.pdf.

Bentley, B. 2013. "Lasting Legacy: J.B. Hunt Transport Continues Tradition of Innovation Created by Its Founder More Than 50 Years Ago." Best DriverJOBS, August.

Berger, P. 2009. "For Sale: $20 Million Particle Accelerator, Never Used." Wired.com, September 9. https://www.wired.com/2009/09/super-collider-gallery/.

Doler, K. 2021. "This Is Why J.B. Hunt Is A Leader in ESG Investing Now." *Investor's Business Daily*, October 26. https://www.investors.com/news/esg-investing-role-model-transportation-hunt/.

Doler, K. 2022. "IBD's 100 Best ESG Companies For 2022." *Investor's Business Daily*, October 24. https://www.investors.com/news/esg-companies-list-top-100-esg-stocks-2022/?es_id=308955a88b.

Hurt, E. 2016. "Hunt Bound for Hall of Fame." *Arkansas Democrat-Gazette*, September 25.

JBHT (J.B. Hunt Transport Services). 2016. "J.B. Hunt Origins 1927–1990." YouTube video, 15:46. www.youtube.com/watch?v=TjfHchzNuQY.

JBHT. 2020. "J.B. Hunt 2020 Sustainability Report." https://www.jbhunt.com/our -company/environmental-sustainability.

Jouzaitis, C. 1989. "Santa Fe, J. B. Hunt Sign Pact." *Chicago Tribune*, December 13.

Patowary, K. 2011. "The Abandoned Remains of the Superconducting Super Collider." https://www.amusingplanet.com/2010/12/abandoned-remains-of-superconducting .html.

Schwartz, M. 1992. *J. B. Hunt: The Long Haul to Success.* Fayetteville: University of Arkansas Press.

Thompson, K., and M. Waller. 2019. *Purple on The Inside: How J.B. Hunt Transport Set Itself Apart in a Field Full of Brown Cows.* Fayetteville, AR: Epic Books.

The Future of Supply Chains

One of the most important lessons we can learn from Hall of Famers like the ones featured in this book is that innovators and innovations are never done. That means the innovations we covered have a future. And while we discussed the future for each innovation at the end of each chapter, there are additional implications and some surprising connections between Hall of Famers that create even more opportunities for further innovation.

Using the supply chain operations reference (SCOR) model—plan, source, make, deliver, and return—and adding in environmental, social, and corporate governance (ESG) as a key aspect working throughout the supply chain as an extension of the return step, we can identify how Hall of Famers build upon each other's innovations and identify further innovation opportunities (Table 7.1).

Make

Henry Ford created a rigorous systematic flow and a standardized product to drive scale and affordability that helped create and grow the car industry.

Toyota's Taiichi Ohno optimized the flow, building upon the Ford production system. Eliyahu Goldratt developed the theory of constraints methodology to remove bottlenecks in processes and flows.

Michael Dell partially moved away from that by reorganizing for mass customization. While scale and optimization were maintained at the module level, a variety of configurations enabled customization of the end product.

Jeff Bezos complemented this with a new, online channel to market. Amazon's wheel of growth still fundamentally seeks scale and

TABLE 7.1 The impact of the Hall of Famers on supply chain operations

Make	Source	Deliver	Plan	Return/ESG
Standardize (Ford)	Integrate (Stephenson, Ford)	Create modes and tools (Stephenson, Raymond, McClean, Casey, Smith)	Project (Stephenson)	Industrialize (Stephenson, Ford)
Optimize (Ohno, Goldratt)	Outsource (Drucker, Ohno)	Improve safety (Dole)	Internal (Ford)	Internalize (Dole)
Reorganize channels and propositions to customers (Dell, Bezos)	Globalize (Dell)	Establish interconnectivity (Hunt)	Supply chain (Ohno, Dell)	Externalize (Menzies, Fritz)
What's next?				
Servitize and digitize	Reshore	Introduce new modes and tools	Dynamic combination between planning and responding	Revolutionize

volume to fund affordability but also to drive expansion of range and offerings.

Extrapolating from that, the future of "make" will likely involve greater levels of servitization and digitization. Both services and physical products include greater and greater levels of automation and technology (look at today's Ford cars), but services are also key drivers of value beyond the product. Amazon provides a channel enabled by technology, and its logistical service is one of its main competitive weapons.

Source

George Stephenson integrated an industry around railroad development and deployed that entire industry in every build project he ran. Ford, meanwhile, built a completely integrated supply chain, all the way up to cotton farms.

Peter Drucker offered outsourcing as an alternative approach that featured prominently in Ohno's lean production model and also made it into later generations of the Ford supply chain. With outsourcing and the conquering of logistics as the "last dark continent," in the words of Drucker, globalization became feasible and massively adopted by Dell and others.

Some companies are now reshoring to regain a level of visibility and control that the original Ford model had, in order to improve their responsiveness to markets and to reduce their risks. This promising pathway for the future also holds ESG benefits. Reshoring creates economic inclusion in the regions where companies sell and reduces the length of the global transportation pipeline, thereby reducing pressure on the transportation system and decreasing emissions.

Deliver

Stephenson (railways), George Raymond (pallets and the pallet jack), Malcolm McLean (shipping), James Casey (UPS), and Fred Smith (FedEx) all created delivery technologies and modalities.

Elizabeth Dole, meanwhile, improved the safety of the delivery system and promoted seatbelts and air bags as technology enhancements. And J.B. Hunt's intermodal business established greater levels of interconnectivity between technologies and modes of transportation.

Technologies around drones and automated guided vehicles (AGVs) are examples of how we are continuing to see new modes and tools, large and small, entering the transportation industry. This builds on Hunt's mindset of creating a technologycentric company.

Plan

Stephenson and his fellow railway builders planned projects in great detail, ultimately connecting railways across multiple projects to create the railway network.

Ford moved planning from projects to the internal organizational level, something that Ohno and Dell expanded to the supply chain level, post outsourcing.

In the future, we will likely move toward a digital-enabled hybrid approach that combines digital cockpits and control towers that help simulate responses within plans.

If the COVID-19 pandemic reinforced anything, it would be that you cannot plan everything or develop a perfect plan. For this reason, a dynamic combination between planning and responding, enabled by technology, will likely provide future innovation.

ESG

Environmental, social, and corporate governance (ESG) may be a newer term, but its principles are far from new.

Ford promoted inclusive employment opportunities and worker safety.

Stephenson enabled economic progress across communities.

J. B. Hunt's intermodal was also an environmentally friendly transportation option *avant la lettre*. Intermodal takes a lot of trucks off the road and thereby reduces the carbon impact of transportation in significant ways.

Dole internalized the ability to use a supply chain for good with the ten-point plan, which aimed to create more opportunities for women and grow diversity and inclusion.

John Menzies's American Logistics Aid Network (ALAN) aims to unleash supply chain capabilities in industry to externally support responses to disaster and embed into industry a focus on using those capabilities for good. ALAN as an organization brings together supply chain providers and expertise in an effort to mitigate the impact of disasters. Lynn Fritz's Institute equally seeks to bring the strength and the best practices of logistics to humanitarian efforts.

While the industry has made great progress toward improved sustainability in supply chains, most leaders would say it has been part of a journey with one step at a time and a long way still to go. In the future, the focus on embedding and improving supply chains as a force for good may gather greater speed, and more revolutionary approaches may emerge.

Implications for Us?

Reflecting upon the successes and contributions of CSCMP Supply Chain Hall of Famers brings us back to the opening epigraphs about seeking wisdom and leading by serving.

CSCMP Supply Chain Hall of Famers sought out wisdom to create new capability, technology, business solutions, and practices. In doing so they served our profession, their customers, businesses, and the many people they worked with as leaders. The massive amount of impact they have had, and still have today, goes well beyond their personal agenda; it was not about them or their personal success to begin with, and it ended up going well beyond the initially targeted impact.

Intermodal, for example, did not start as an environmentally friendly mode of transportation, but it is. Bar codes were developed for the grocery store checkout process, not to enable traceability of medical suppliers or as a vehicle for consumer information provision, but they did end up doing that. The ten-plan program for improving the diversity of the DOT was developed for the DOT, but President Reagan suggested his other agencies adopt the program also. So clearly those that seek out wisdom can find her, and those that serve more lead more and those that humble themselves will go first when it comes to impact and contribution. So how does that translate to us the readership of this book?

Academics

Academics have the privileged opportunity to generate societal value; hence it is not surprising that so many academic thought leaders have been inducted into the CSCMP Supply Chain Hall of Fame as Distinguished Service Award recipients. The critical questions that academics can ask themselves and each other based upon the lessons of Hall of Famers include:

- Are you seeking wisdom in your research or are you just seeking promotion and status?
- Do you publish research that effectively shares wisdom and has impact by serving as input to other research or managerial efforts? Or are you publishing for the check in the box, even though nobody may ever read it, making it a gift that was not given, not a gift that keeps on giving?
- And what about societal impact? Did you lift a finger for supply chain progress during the pandemic? Do you seek to understand innovative opportunities in industry for the good of progress in the profession

or are you seeking academic justification of your niche in the body of knowledge?

- Do you teach to share wisdom or teach to hit your minimum load requirements?
- When you teach do you seek to serve so that students can soar, or seek to have students pass your course (even when that may be the only thing needed for a positive student evaluation)?

Academic Administrators

Academic administrators face a challenging leadership setting: partially self-governed organizations with lots of committees, a broad group of stakeholders, and a challenging economic environment for education and research—but what to do with that position? Be a scribe or a servant leader seeking wisdom?

- Do you let bureaucratic aspects rule your agenda and time spend, or do you navigate those aspects, like business leaders do when navigating complex market environments? And do you seek to innovate and create service opportunities to win in your markets for students, talent, and wisdom?
- Are you letting faculty serve more if they want to and are you supporting the quest for wisdom irrespective of rank, tenure, or position so that all that seek can find? Or are you reducing course overloads and access to research funding based upon rank or type of faculty? Are you being selective in providing access to funding and support based upon position, not based upon the desire to seek out wisdom and service?
- Are you putting weight on people or are you leading by taking on the weight of others and clearing a path for as many as possible?
- Do you stand in line when policy, procedure, and formalities come into play or do you humble yourself in search of innovative service opportunities, even if it means lifting the yoke of others?
- Are you seeking a seat at the leadership table (equivalent to the "banquet") and performing "duties to be seen" or are you serving faulty, students, and society, even if that means finding innovative ways to do just that?

Managers

Many academic journal articles in the field of management include a section on implications for managers, and many managers engage with peers and universities to learn and to seek talent. Some of the original CSCMP Distinguished Service Award recipients, such as Don Bowersox, came from industry to go into academia in their quest for wisdom and opportunities to serve and create the field. Others, like Martin Christopher, have role modeled the value of close industry relationships and engagement to inform research and innovation. In support of managers seeking wisdom and opportunities to support supply chain innovation for the good of their business and the profession, here are some suggestions:

- Are you seeking wisdom by engaging with researchers? Are you sharing your wisdom with researchers and are you also sharing wisdom you seek with researchers that can help you find her?
- Are you engaging with students that are seeking wisdom? It is a great way to serve the talent of the future outside and inside your organization, but please do not only approach it as a hiring pipeline initiative—by supporting leaders of the future you may be contributing to the path of the next Hall of Famer, even if you may humble your own organization in the process.
- As a manager you have authority and you can "take a seat at the banquet," but are you using your position to your personal advantage or putting it to use in service of others and the quest for wisdom?
- Are you making the quest for wisdom safe in your organization like Henry Ford did?

The Key to the Future? You!

None of the supply chain industry's potential will come to fruition without capable and driven leaders.

Talent explains the gap between potential and delivered results and value. Talent explains the gap between OK and best-in-class performance. And talent propels innovation forward. So beyond the talents of the Hall of Famers we have learned from in this book, it is the talent of aspiring and current supply chain managers that is most crucial to the industry's future.

This is why CSCMP focuses not only on connecting but also on educating and developing supply chain professionals during the lifecycle of their careers. And, personally, it is why I came back from industry to teach. By exciting, equipping, and educating leaders of the future, I get the opportunity to serve the profession that has been so good to me in an area of great need.

In the main room of the CSCMP Supply Chain Hall of Fame building, we have a wall devoted to quotes from supply chain students. We asked about their supply chain dreams and aspirations, and they painted an exciting, bright picture with their words. We can all feel encouraged by the dreams and aspirations shared in these types of statements:

- "My dream for the future of supply chain is to utilize more sustainable practices throughout the entire business that would help make the world a better place without leaving a significant ecological footprint."
- "My dream for supply chain is to see a larger number of females leading and representing the industry—and just looking around the class, it's looking promising."
- "Supply chain is exciting to me because of the idea that there is no universal solution. This allows for continual innovation that is only limited by our own ideas."
- "It is my dream for supply chain to continue to improve technology, have advanced data acquisition, and seamless knowledge transfer among all aspects of the supply chain end-to-end."
- "A way for a business to improve is by really focusing on its relationships with suppliers and customers."

An obvious consequence of these aspirations, beyond hope for the future, is that hiring managers who recruit this talent had better be ready to support, train, accommodate, and get out of the way while they run with it!

So, who will be the next CSCMP Supply Chain Hall of Fame innovator?

Who will transform the industry and propel supply chain management forward?

Could it be you?

Epilogue

Voices at the Table

When this book was near completion, I asked Donna Palumbo-Miele and Rob Haddock for their reflections on the lessons we can learn from the Hall of Famers featured in these pages and then to share their thoughts about what those lessons mean for the future of supply chain and what it might imply for students of the supply chain. Both Donna and Rob have served CSCMP and our profession for many years, and their words of encouragement for supply chain managers of today and the future will hopefully help inspire many, including new Hall of Famers!

Pushing the Limits

As we witness the evolution and transformation of the supply chain profession, it is clear the creativity, innovation, and ingenuity of those in the field have been the driving force behind advancements across the entire ecosystem. And as this book demonstrates, the profession continues to show remarkable potential when we push the limits of what is possible.

I come from a family of coal miners. So, I am particularly inspired by the innovative thinking and execution that allowed my grandfather and father to perform their jobs in the coal mines of central Pennsylvania and transport coal to regions across the country. We see this same kind of ingenuity and determination at work in the supply chain profession, where individuals and teams work tirelessly to overcome complex challenges and achieve breakthrough results.

We have seen how much modern society depends on a well-functioning supply chain. The fact that we often take it for granted that goods and services arrive smoothly is a testament to the hard work of millions around the world each day.

Of course, innovation takes time. When we see the most creative and impactful forms of innovation among teams that work together as one, the results can be truly transformative. Thanks to the collaboration and coordination between internal teams and external partners, industry pioneers have successfully addressed some of the most complex challenges within supply chain management. As the examples in this book remind us, innovation in the industry has connected our modern society and made it a safer, more prosperous, and better place.

Looking ahead, we know supply chain resiliency and transparency will continue to be top priorities for consumers and companies. By seeking to understand these needs and leveraging, advancing, and enabling technologies, we can make informed decisions and drive strategy in the most effective way possible. The implementation of standardization will also play a crucial role in driving productivity and enabling continuous improvement in functions and processes.

Perhaps most important is the need to upskill talent and ensure that we are empowering the next generation of supply chain professionals with the fresh perspectives and relevant skills necessary for continuous transformation. With agility, talent, and a commitment to continuous learning, we can add even more value to the profession and the communities we serve.

It is my hope that this book will serve as a valuable resource for those looking to stay at the forefront of supply chain innovation and make a real difference in the world. There is so much inspiration we can draw from the pioneers highlighted in these pages who have paved the path that brought us to where we are today.

Even with all the technology at our fingertips, it has been the people behind the technology who have reimagined what is possible in supply chain management. Their examples compel us to continue raising the bar, setting our standards higher, and pushing the envelope in innovation. By sharing insights, best practices, and real-world examples, we can continue to push the boundaries of what is possible and achieve truly remarkable results.

Donna Palumbo-Miele
Founder and CEO of Concordia
Supply Chain Group
2025 Chair of the CSCMP Board of
Directors

Four Issues for the Future

Spending four decades supporting the supply chain of one of the best-known brands on the planet gave me a front row seat to innovations and advancements in the industry that were well beyond my comprehension in the early 1980s.

The idea of colleges and universities across the globe educating the young minds on the principles of end-to-end (E2E) supply chain disciplines would have been considered revolutionary back then. Procurement, economics, and management degrees were the extent of the higher education opportunities, and there was little understanding of the interdependencies across the various disciplines needed to drive a competitive advantage supply chain mind-set.

Throughout my career I've been able to work across industries with the best supply chain professionals to assist educators in building curriculums for the future. These experiences, along with what I learned on the job, have provided a few insights into the future of the discipline.

For instance, I'm convinced that those entering the profession need to take a diverse approach to their career road map and keep an open and innovative mind-set about their work.

I never had goals of reaching a certain level by a certain time in my career, but two core values proved key to my personal development: A strong work ethic (I spent ten years as a paperboy growing up) and intellectual curiosity (always ask "Why?" and "Is there a better way?"). Demonstrating those traits led to diverse opportunities and experiences in lateral moves and advancements across the supply chain.

Credibility comes with experience, and it can come in a range of areas—production, warehousing, customer service, demand and supply planning, transportation, or interacting with business team leaders. The more exposure and experience, the easier it gets to connect the dots and suggest how to resolve the greatest supply chain challenges.

It's also worth remembering that supply chains come in all shapes and sizes. Even with the advances in education providing foundational knowledge, each company's supply chain is tied to consumer behavior economics, strategic inefficiencies, and varying levels of supply chain understanding and investment by the company's C-suite leaders.

New supply chain professionals may be armed with best practice theories and supported by state-of-the-art technologies, but don't be surprised or alarmed if your new employer has a few supply chain inefficiencies. Take the approach that you got there just in time to make them a better company!

To either achieve or maintain a competitive advantage, supply chain leaders will need to focus on issues that can be summed up in four areas:

1. **Designing supply chains with flexibility, resiliency, and sustainability.** The go-to market strategies for modern companies are constantly adjusting to maintain consumer relevance. Since most supply chains involve capital, yesterday's great innovation can be outdated tomorrow and suddenly face growing productivity challenges. Supply chain professionals are called on to constantly uncover the solutions that will yield the highest service at the optimal costs and that are critical to achieving profitability.

2. **Investing wisely in technology.** Technology is an enabler and companies must invest in it wisely and methodically to ensure personnel benefit. In many cases, the promise of plug-and-play integration falls short without successful change management, and technology failures can destroy customer satisfaction and drive companies out of business. Investments in people and process must occur in parallel to any advances in technology.

3. **Mining data for insights.** In an era of "big data" and "data lakes," too many companies are what I term "data rich" and "insight poor." Information systems now generate millions of bytes of information weekly, but the supply chain still lacks the ability to gain insights from that data on how to adjust future business strategies. With the evolution of high-power visualization software, companies must train internal resources or partner with providers that can help make sense of all the noise via dynamic alerts, control towers, and other tools.

4. **Documenting and training.** Finally, many companies struggle with process documentation and training of new people, which eventually results in old problems resurfacing after a few

organizational changes. Fortunately, electronic archiving makes critical processes accessible to the masses so they no longer get lost on a dusty bookshelf in the office of someone who has departed the company. But discipline is still needed for the knowledge holder to share and create the electronic imaginary, although companies are getting wiser about its value and focusing more time on legacy documents.

In closing, supply chains are at the foundation of almost every company, and the profession is finally being recognized for the value it adds in supporting modern lifestyles. Visionaries of the past have laid the foundations, readying those who are already in and just entering the field to develop the best supply chains the world has ever experienced. That's why I am so excited for the future of supply chains.

Rob Haddock
Former Group Director for Transportation Strategy, the Coca-Cola Company 2026 Chair of the CSCMP Board of Directors

CSCMP Hall of Famers

 Note: New members are inducted annually. An updated version of this list is available on the CSCMP website at https://cscmp.org/CSCMP/Awards/CSCMP_Supply _Chain_Hall_of_Fame.aspx.

2023 Inductee
- Lynn Fritz, founder of the Fritz Institute for Humanitarian Logistics and former Chairman and CEO of Fritz Companies

2022 Inductee
- Beth Ford, President and CEO of Land O'Lakes and former Chief Supply Chain Officer (CSCO) of Land O'Lakes

2021 Inductee
- John Menzies, founder of the American Logistics Aid Network (ALAN)

2020 Inductee
- Taiichi Ohno, creator of the Toyota Production System

2019 Inductees
- James Casey, founder and former Chairman of UPS
- Elizabeth Dole, former United States Senator and Secretary of Transportation
- Eliyahu Goldratt, creator of the Theory of Constraints
- George Raymond Sr., inventor of the wooden pallet and pallet jack

2018 Inductees
- Michael Dell, founder of Dell Technologies
- Peter Drucker, knowledge creator as a consultant, educator, and author
- George Stephenson, father of the modern railway system

2017 Inductees
- Jeff Bezos, founder and CEO of Amazon
- George Lauer, innovator of the Universal Product Code (UPC)

2016 Inductees
- Henry Ford, pioneer of assembly line production
- Johnnie Bryan (J. B.) Hunt, pioneer of intermodal partnerships between railroads and trucking
- Malcom McLean, developer of the modern standardized shipping container

CSCMP Distinguished Service Award Recipients

 Note: New members are inducted annually. An updated version of this list is available on the CSCMP website at https://cscmp.org/CSCMP/Awards/Distinguished _Service_Award.aspx.

2023: Dr. Ted Stank, Professor, University of Tennessee

2022: Masao Nishi, Principal of Nishi Strategic Advisory and former CSCO of Sysco Corporation

2021: Dr. Dale Rogers, Professor, Arizona State University

2020: Dr. Matthew A. Waller, Dean, Sam M. Walton College of Business, University of Arkansas

2019: Kathy Wengel, Executive Vice President and Chief Global Supply Chain Officer for Johnson & Johnson

2018: Dr. John Gattorna, author, academic, and Principal of Gattorna Alignment

2017: Dr. Nancy Nix, Executive Director of Achieving Women's Excellence in Supply Chain Operations, Management, and Education (AWESOME)

2016: Dr. Chris Caplice, Executive Director of the MIT Center for Transportation and Logistics

2015: Robert Martichenko, CEO, LeanCor Supply Chain Group

2014: Mike Regan, Chief of Relationship Development, TranzAct Technologies, Inc.

2013: Abré Pienaar, CEO, iPlan

2012: Ann Drake, Chairman and CEO, DSC Logistics

2011: Dr. James R. Stock, Frank Harvey Endowed Professor of Marketing, University of South Florida

2010: Charles L. Taylor, founder and Principal, Awake! Consulting

2009: Joel L. Sutherland, Managing Director of Lehigh University's Center for Value Chain Research

2008: Arthur Mesher, CEO, The Descartes Systems Group Inc.

2007: Dr. Thomas W. Speh, Distinguished Professor of Distribution, Miami University

2006: Herbert S. Shear, CEO, GENCO

2005: Dr. Martin G. Christopher, Professor of Marketing and Logistics, Cranfield University, UK

2004: Dr. John Mentzer, Distinguished Professor of Logistics, University of Tennessee

2003: H. Lee Scott, Jr., Chairman, Wal-Mart Corporation

2002: Donald J. Schneider, Chairman, Schneider Logistics, Inc.

2001: Ralph W. Drayer, Vice President, Customer Service and Logistics, Procter & Gamble

1999: Richard F. Powers, President, Insight, Inc.

1998: William C. Copacino, Managing Partner, Andersen Consulting Strategic Services Practice

1997: Dr. Yossi Sheffi, Professor, Massachusetts Institute of Technology

1996: Larry S. Mulkey, President, Ryder Integrated Logistics

1995: Joseph C. Andraski, Vice President Integrated Logistics, Nabisco Inc.

1994: Roger W. Carlson, Executive Vice President, Exel Logistics-North America

1993: Dr. John Langley, John H. Dove Distinguished Professor, University of Tennessee

1992: Howard S. Gochberg, Vice President (retired), Land O'Lakes, Inc.

1991: Dr. John J. Coyle, Executive Director, Center for Logistics Research, Pennsylvania State University

1990: Roger W. Kallock, Chairman, Cleveland Consulting Associates

1989: Frederick W. Smith, CEO/Chairman, Federal Express Corporation

1988: George A. Gecowets, Executive Vice President, Council of Logistics Management

1987: Ronald E. Seger, Vice President, A.T. Kearney, Inc.

1986: Dr. Douglas M. Lambert, Professor of Marketing, University of South Florida

1985: Arthur W. Todd, Director of Purchasing, Lincoln Electric Company

1984: Bob Packwood, United States Senator

1983: Bernard J. Hale, Vice President, Distribution Services, Bergen Brunswig Corporation

1982: Jerome D. Krassenstein, Vice President, Chessie System

1981: Robert V. Delaney, Manager of Distribution, International Paper Company

1980: Clifford F. Lynch, Vice President of Distribution, Quaker Oats Company

1979: Wendell M. Stewart, Vice President, A.T. Kearney, Inc.

1978: Robert J. Franco, Vice Chairman, Spector Industries

1977: Kenneth B. Ackerman, Chairman, Distribution Centers, Inc.

1976: Dr. Bernard J. LaLonde, Professor of Marketing and Logistics, The Ohio State University

1975: Burr W. Hupp, Managing Director, Drake Sheahan/Stewart Dougall

1974: Dr. James L. Heskett, Professor of Business Logistics, Harvard University

1973: Robert E. Schellberg, Vice President, Distribution, Eastman Kodak Company

1972: Warren Blanding, Executive Vice President, Marketing Publications, Inc.

1971: Mark Egan, Tourism Advisor for Turkey

1970: Dr. Gayton E. Germane, Professor of Logistics, Stanford University

1969: Bruce J. Riggs, General Traffic Manager, Norton Company

1968: Dr. Edward W. Smykay, Professor, Michigan State University

1967: E. Grosvenor Plowman, Vice President, Traffic, U.S. Steel

1966: Dr. Donald J. Bowersox, Vice President/General Manager, E.F. MacDonald Stamp Company

1965: Will Gribble, Director, Customer Service, Pillsbury Company

Acknowledgments

Thank you to Stephen Caldwell for being the secret sauce behind this book—you are very talented and see blessings everywhere while it is really you that are the blessing!

Thank you to Mark Baxa, Donna Polumbo-Miele, and Rob Haddock for contributing to this book. As part of the CSCMP community, I have been able to connect and collaborate with supply chain rock stars and trailblazers like you, as well as Adri Pienaar, Nancy Nix, Heather Sheehan, and many others. This has provided great motivation to serve CSCMP through the writing of this book.

Thank you to Martin Christopher and Don Bowersox for being role models for how academia can be relevant, innovative, timely, and engaged with industry, and for making progress in the discipline that you helped start. Thank you for inspiring and equipping me. Hopefully my work can make a modest contribution to honoring your model while inspiring others the way you inspired me.

Thank you to Alan Harrison for pioneering a path from industry back into academia. I followed in your footsteps, and I remain grateful for our collaboration on your book *Logistics Management and Strategy*, which has impacted so many who have gone into our field. I hope this book will further contribute to that impact.

Thank you to the many supply chain and procurement professionals I have had the pleasure of working with and for. The opportunities we captured—and even some that we did not—inspire me to serve our profession through teaching, research, and service, outside the reach of the corporate shortcomings such as politics, hierarchies, egos, and a lack of vision or ambitions. (Not that those don't exist in academia, of course.)

Thank you to the many executives who help me teach and research. The passion and experience you bring to the classroom and the innovative practices you let me capture in my research provide the bedrock for progress and innovation in areas outlined in this book. Beyond the areas where you already grant me the privilege of supporting you, I hope this book can further your efforts for progress. I owe particular gratitude to Michael DeWitt and team, Russ Stewart and team, Dominique Lebigot and team, Thomas Udesen, and Bruno Vaffier.

I also would like to thank Anja and Henk van Hoek for encouraging me to find my path. I ended up in supply chain and procurement because it fulfilled my aspiration for an international setting with lots of opportunities for business and societal progress, where there never is a dull day and where there's always an opportunity to serve and contribute. The field has been incredibly good to me. Your pride and that of Cathy and Bob Weissblatt has encouraged me on a path that has included a task as daunting as writing about the greatest innovators and leaders in supply chain history.

Finally, everyone who knows me also knows that, thanks to Maryl, I married up. And my boys know that they have given me more than I can ever give them. Thank you for loving me as much as you do and for supporting me. All four of you are living proof of the fact that God is incredibly good!

About the CSCMP Supply Chain Hall of Fame

The Council of Supply Chain Management Professionals (CSCMP) was founded in 1963 and launched its Hall of Fame in 2016 to celebrate, recognize, and archive the achievements of the discipline's innovators and groundbreaking leaders.

Initially, the CSCMP Supply Chain Hall of Fame was exclusively online and new inductees were added at each year's conference. In 2019, however, former board chair Remko van Hoek proposed a plan for a physical hall of fame, and the board approved it.

The generosity of Johnelle Hunt (cofounder of J.B. Hunt Transport), Gus Blass III (general partner of Capital Properties LLC), and Alex Blass (a partner in Sage Partners LLC) resulted in space for the hall on the top floor of the newly constructed Northgate Building in Rogers, Arkansas.

The facility, which opened in 2020, is located in the hub of innovation in supply chain management. It is within a few miles of the headquarters of J.B. Hunt Transport, Walmart, dozens of other companies with supply chain expertise, and the Sam M. Walton College of Business at the University of Arkansas, which offers top-ranked supply chain programs.

The Walton College hosts the Hall of Fame, with Remko van Hoek, a professor of supply chain, serving as executive director. In addition to space for rotating exhibits, the facility holds seminars, CSCMP Roundtables and meetings, work sessions, lectures, and inductee events.

Learn more about that Hall of Fame at https://walton.uark.edu/departments/supplychain/hall-of-fame/.

Index

Note: figures and tables are denoted by *f* and *t,* respectively.

BNSF (Burlington Northern Santa Fe),
122, 129
Bowersox, Don, 5, 141
Bragg, Janet Waterford, 108
Brandywine Iron Works, 105
Bridgwood, Charlotte, 106
Bristol Meyers, 58
Brown, Willa, 107
"Building B," Ford and, 39–40
bullwhip effect, 49, 50–51
Burke, Alinda, 110
Burlington Northern, 122
Burns, Beverly, 110
Bush, George H. W., 79, 90, 104
Business Week (magazine), 65

C

Canadian National Railway, 123, 133
carbon calculator, 127, 128
Carbon Diet services, 127–28
Casey, James, 6, 136*t*, 137
Christopher, Martin, 4, 141
Cischke, Sue, 112
Civil Aeronautics Administration, 108
Civil Air Patrol, 107
Claybrook, Joan, 110
CLEAN Transport carbon calculator,
127, 128
coal mining, Stephenson and development of
railway system and, 16, 17, 18–19, 25, 29
Coast Guard, Dole and, 80
Cochran, Jacqueline, 108
Coleman, Bessie, 107
collaboration, success and, 47
Collins, David, 74, 75
Collins, Eileen, 111
Commercial Motor Vehicle Safety Act
(1986), 93
Computer Identics Corporation, 74, 75
Conrail, 99, 122
constraints methodology, 135
consumer value, cost saving and, 68
containers, standardization of, 8, 28, 120,
124, 128, 136*t*, 137
continuous improvement: Ford and, 42–43;
Ohno and Goldratt and, 9; Stephenson
and, 25
continuous learning, importance of, 144

Converse, Mary, 107–8
Corominas, Albert, 41
cost saving, consumer value and, 68
cotton industry, effect of development of rail
system on, 19, 23, 29*t*
Council for Supply Chain Management
Professionals (CSCMP), 3, 4; Bowersox
and, 5; focus of, 142; Hall of Fame, 5–6
Council of Logistics Management (CLM), 5
Cover, Beverly, 109
COVID-19 pandemic: global supply chains
and, 11; importance of supply chain and,
3; people skills and management during,
101; planning and, 138
credibility, career success and, 145
Crouse, David, 61
CSX Transportation, 123
culture, at J.B. Hunt Transport, 125
customer value and service, Ford and, 42
customization, Dell and, 8, 45

D

Danahar Corporation, 102
Darlington to Stockton rail line, Stephenson
and, 19–20, 26, 27, 32
DataBar, 77
DataMatrix codes, 72
data mining for insights, 146
data storage, UPC and, 68
Davies, Hunter, 17
Death and Life of Great American Cities, The
(Jacobs), 109
DeBusk, Johnelle, 116, 117*f. See also* Hunt,
Johnelle DeBusk
deliver, SCOR model and, 136*t*, 137
delivery, Ford and, 48, 48*t*
Dell, Michael, 37; Ford and, 45; globalization
and, 136*t*, 137; lean production and, 9;
mass customization and, 8, 45, 135
demand responsiveness, of Ford production
system, 44
Dennis, Olive, 106–7
Denso, 70
Department of Transportation (DOT). *See
also* Dole, Elizabeth Hanford: employee
recognition at, 99–100; increase in
opportunities for women under Dole's
management, 83–90

impact beyond original design, 69; teamwork and, 67; time for, 67, 144
in-plant logistics, Ford and, 48–49
integration, 136*t*
intermodal logistics, 8, 11, 139; Hunt and, 6,
116, 118–25, 123*f*; relevance of, 128–29
International Journal of Physical Distribution
(IJPD), 4
International Truck and Engine Corporation,
111
Investor's Business Daily (journal), Best ESG
Companies, 124–25
ITF-14 bar codes, 77

J

Jacobs, Jane, 109
J.B. Hunt Company, 118, 132
J.B. Hunt Intermodal, 122–23
J.B. Hunt Transport (JBHT). *See also* Hunt,
Johnnie Bryan (J. B.): environment,
sustainability, and, 127–28; expansion
of, 132–33; intermodal logistics and,
11, 122–25; partnership with Santa Fe
Railway, 132; as public corporation, 118;
taken public, 132
J.B. Hunt Transport Services, 115
*Journal of Purchasing (Journal of Supply Chain
Management)*, 4
just-in-time production, Ford and, 37, 44–45

K

kanban card, 70*f*
Kansas City Southern/Kansas City Southern
in Mexico, 123
Kansas City Southern Railway Company
(KCS), 129
Kevlar, 109
Kidder, Sarah Clark, 106
Killingworth High Pit coal mine,
Stephenson and, 16, 18, 32
King, Charles Brady, 36, 52
Kroger supermarket chain, 60, 69, 75, 76
Kwolek, Stephanie Louise, 109

L

labor productivity, Ford and, 48*t*
LaLonde, Bernard (Bud), 4
Lanham, Mazie, 108
Larkin, John, 129–30

laser: bar code technology and, 57–58; development of, 74
Laurer, George, 6, 55–78; on adoption of UPC,
65–66; contemporary relevance, 70–71;
development of bar code technology and, 7,
8, 10, 56–63; drive for adoption of bar code
and, 64–66; exemplification of principles,
66–69; on fresh perspective and innovation, 69; future bar code developments,
71–73; industry consortium and development of bar code, 58–69; links to supply
chain innovators, 69–70; McEnroe and,
60, 61; standard setting and, 28; timeline,
73–77; on UPC demonstrating viability of
bar codes, 70; Woodland and, 61, 63
Laurer, Marilyn, 66
leadership: Dole's inclusive style of, 80; Ford
and best practices in, 46–47
League of Railway Industry Women, 111
lean production: bar codes and QR codes
and, 70; Ford and, 37; Ohno and, 9, 44,
136–37
legal drinking age, Dole and, 91
Leicester and Swannington Railway, 21
lifelong learning: Ford and need for, 7, 47, 51;
modern supply chains and, 30
Lightner, Candy, 110
Linde, 125
Livermore, Ann, 111
Liverpool to Manchester line, Stephenson
and, 19, 21, 32
"Locomotion No. 1": model of at Henry Ford
Museum, 28; Stephenson and, 19, 20*f*
locomotive power, compared to horsepower,
20, 21*f*
locomotives: growth in production and batch
size in UK, 23–26, 24*f*, 26*f*; invention of,
19, 25
Lukens, Rebecca, 105

M

Mack Avenue Plant (Ford), 52
Madsen Enterprises, 58
mail carried by rail, 19, 22, 29*t*
Maiman, Theodore, 57, 69, 74
make, in SCOR model, 135–36, 136*t*
managers, questions for, 141
manufacturing, Ford's wholistic approach
to, 42

About the Author

Remko van Hoek is a professor of practice in the Sam M. Walton College of Business at the University of Arkansas (nontenured, one-year appointment) and the executive director of the Council of Supply Chain Management Professionals (CSCMP) Supply Chain Hall of Fame. Remko has extensive experience in the corporate and academic worlds. The former chief procurement officer for the Walt Disney Company has held senior supply chain executive roles in the United States and Europe at several companies, including Nike and PwC. And he previously taught as a professor and/or visiting professor at the Cranfield School of Management in England, the Rotterdam School of Management in the Netherlands, and the Vlerick School of Management in Belgium. He advises companies around the world on procurement and has served CSCMP on committees and its board for over two decades.

He serves on seven editorial advisory boards, was European editor of *International Journal of Physical Distribution and Logistics Management* (IJPDLM), and has more than one hundred publications in international peer-reviewed journals, including *Journal of Operations Management, Journal of Business Logistics, Sloan Management Review,* and *Harvard Business Review.* He also holds a fellowship from the Chartered Institute of Logistics and Transport (CILT) and the Chartered Institute of Procurement and Supply (CIPS), both in the United Kingdom.

Remko, who earned a PhD in international economics from Utrecht University in the Netherlands, is coauthor of *Integrating Blockchain into Supply Chain Management* (Kogan Page, 2019), *Logistics Management and Strategy* (Pearson Education, 2024, 7th edition, translated into seven languages), and *Leading Procurement Strategy* (Kogan Page, 2025, 4th edition, translated into two languages). Remko won the MBA teacher of the year award in 2018 and the Best All Around Faculty Award of the Sam M. Walton College of Business in 2022, and he received a research fellowship from the Dole Institute of Politics for the period 2020–2022. He is the only person who is on the top ten list of thought leaders in supply chain as well as the author of one of the top ten textbooks in supply chain and the top ten books for executives in supply chain. He is in the top 2 percent of the most referenced authors in business and management sciences (2024) and is one of only seven Walton College scholars in the top 1,500 business and management scholars on the 2024 research.com list. He has won numerous awards for his research and contributions, including a record three Plowman Best Paper Awards from CSCMP.